Catherine Marshall

Adventures in Prayer

Catherine Marshall
Adventures in Prayer

ILLUSTRATIONS BY NED GLATTAUER

Published by
chosen books
Distributed by Fleming H. Revell Company
Old Tappan, New Jersey

Scripture quotations not otherwise identified are from the King James Version of the Bible.

Scripture quotations identified MOFFATT are from THE BIBLE: A NEW TRANSLATION by James Moffatt. Copyright 1954 by James A. R. Moffatt. By permission of Harper & Row, Publishers, Inc.

Scripture quotations identified LB are from The Living Bible, Copyright © 1971 by Tyndale House Publishers, Wheaton, Illinois 60187. All rights reserved.

Scripture quotations identified PHILLIPS are from THE NEW TESTAMENT IN MODERN ENGLISH (Revised Edition), translated by J. B. Phillips. © J. B. Phillips, 1958, 1960, 1972. Used by permission of Macmillan Publishing Co., Inc.

Scripture quotations identified RSV are from the Revised Standard Version of the Bible, copyrighted 1946, 1952, © 1971 and 1973.

Edited material which is reprinted from and under copyright by Guideposts Associates, Inc. is used by permission.

Excerpt from *The Practice of the Presence of God* by Brother Lawrence is used by permission of Fleming H. Revell Company.

Excerpt from *Love Is an Everyday Thing* by Colleen Townsend Evans is used by permission of Fleming H. Revell Company.

Excerpt from *A Moveable Feast* by Ernest Hemingway is used by permission of Charles Scribner's Sons.

Excerpt from *The Healing Light* by Agnes Sanford is used by permission of Macalester Park Publishing Company.

Excerpt from *Livingstone's African Journal 1853–1856*, edited by Isaac Schapera, is used by permission of Chatto and Windus, Ltd.

Excerpt from C. S. Lewis: *The Screwtape Letters* (© C. S. Lewis, 1942) is used by permission of Macmillan Publishing Co., Inc.

Library of Congress Cataloging in Publication Data

Marshall, Catherine Wood, date
    Adventures in prayer.
    1. Prayer. 2. Prayers. I. Title.
BV210.2.M35   248'.3   75-15720
ISBN 0-912376-09-0

CONTENTS

PROLOGUE

Admittance to the School of Prayer is by an entrance test with only two questions. The first one is: Are you in real need? The second is: Do you admit that you are helpless to handle that need?

Whatever I have learned about prayer has come as the result of times when I could answer a resounding *yes* to both questions. Looking back over my life, those times of need stand out like mountain peaks rather than, as one might suppose, valleys of despond. Peaks—because each time I learned something important about God—how real He is and how gloriously able to answer prayer.

In childhood one of those times of learning came through my desperate fear of the dark. In my teens, there was the dire need of funds for college. What I learned then I share in "The Prayer That Helps Your Dreams Come True."

At twenty-seven the need was a serious illness. There the mountain-peak learning was "The Prayer of Relinquishment."

The peak in my thirties was the gigantic one of my husband Peter Marshall's sudden death, along with lesser hills of need: how to rear a son without his father, how to find a career for

7

myself at this point in life and without any specialized training. During that era I was taught "The Claiming Prayer."

Years later, after my marriage to Leonard LeSourd and the taking on of three young children, it was back to the School of Prayer again. As usual, there was no problem about passing the entrance test; my need was great, my inadequacy obvious. Out of these years came "The Prayer of Helplessness."

More often, of course, the situation that drove me to my knees was not so intensely personal. The need might be a friend's—or one I had only read about somewhere in our war-torn and hungry world. But always the criteria held: great needs and insufficient resources of my own with which to meet them.

In time I shared many of my prayer discoveries in the pages of *Guideposts* magazine. Eventually, a booklet of six prayer articles was put together. There has been a continuous demand for it ever since. Recently, I was asked to edit this material for a more permanent small book. Editing was necessary because each article had been condensed and shortened to fit *Guideposts'* necessarily limited space. Thus in the pages that follow, there appears for the first time the complete original text of the six prayer articles. This material falls into the category of a "classic" only in the sense that it has already been time-tested in print.

In addition, since new times are already bringing new lessons in prayer, I have added two new chapters, "Prayer Is Asking" and "The Waiting Prayer."

I have also written for this book a special prayer to follow each chapter. All of us have days when prayer seems to flow effortlessly, spontaneously. At other times the burden of our hearts needs help in finding its way to our lips, and it is for such moments that these prayers are offered—not as a substitute for our individual petitions, but as a launching pad for them.

Of course, no lifetime and no book, even one many times the length of this one, can do more than skim the surface of a subject as vast and all-encompassing as prayer. In this volume I have nowhere mentioned even the little I know about prayer as adoration—thanksgiving—praise—contemplation—meditation—or simply the lifting of the human heart in silent communion with the Lover of our souls. This is not because I consider such dimensions of prayer unimportant—quite the contrary—but because down through the centuries writers far more qualified than I have left us classics of instruction in their use.

What I have found strangely lacking in my own times of need are guidelines to prayer at its humblest and most basic: prayer as *asking*. The prayer of a child quite simply running to its father for help. This is what we would rediscover in an age of perplexity—how do we run to the Father?

In the seventies, the halls and classrooms of the School of Prayer are crowded as never before because our needs press upon us with new urgency: worldwide economic crises, marriage problems on the rise, a widening generation gap, drug addiction, alcoholism, cancer of almost epidemic frequency. No wonder we rush to school! Our thirst is deep, our eagerness to learn is enormous.

What good news it is that our very inadequacy is the master key swinging wide the door to His adequacy. Forever and forever our thirst and hunger drive us to "taste and see that the Lord is good." Who but Jesus could ever have thought of a plan like that!

CATHERINE MARSHALL
March, 1975

CHAPTER ONE

PRAYER IS ASKING

Recently a friend told me this incident. . . . Her daughter Elizabeth had taken a summer job wrapping meat in a supermarket to earn money for college. Just before time to leave for work one morning, Elizabeth missed one of her contact lenses. Though her mother joined in the search, the lens was nowhere to be found.

After Elizabeth had left for work wearing her regular glasses, her mother sat sipping a cup of coffee, thinking about their little crisis. There were a thousand and one places that tiny teardrop of plastic could have lodged. Then she wondered: should she pray about this? Was it too trivial? This friend, Tib Sherrill, had always had a special horror of prayers which treated the Lord of the Universe like a bellhop or a celestial Santa Claus.

Yet Tib knew that to replace the lens would cost Elizabeth a week's salary—money she was counting on for school needs. There would also be a week of sniffles from the refrigerated room where she worked, and of burnt fingers from the hot sealing wire.

Into my friend's mind came the remembrance of the parable which Jesus had told about a woman searching for one lost silver coin—a valuable one.[1] "The story shows," she mused, "that Jesus cared about such things, not because they are important in themselves, but because they are important to us.

"Yes, Lord," she concluded, "we do need help with this. Will You lead me to the missing lens?"

For no reason she was aware of, she got up and walked to the bathroom. Stooping, she ran her hands carefully through the thick pile of the bathroom rug. No, nothing.

She stood up and glanced at the basin. "Why," she thought, "it could have fallen out here and been washed right down the drain." She lifted out the chrome plunger to peer into the pipe. And there, at the very bottom of the metal plunger tube, was the missing lens, clinging like a tiny droplet of water. The first person to turn on the faucet would have washed it away.

"It had been less than a minute since I made that prayer in the kitchen," Tib told me. "And of all possible places I might have thought to look, it would never in a million years have occurred to me to lift out that plunger."

This mother had experienced answered prayer at its most basic level—asking. We are in need or trouble: a major crisis or a minor one. Taking Jesus at His word that God really is our Father, we come as His child, telling Him our need in the most simple direct way, asking His help.

If any of us has not yet experienced the glory of such a definite answer to prayer, then, as the Apostle James tells us—it's our own fault: ". . . you miss what you want because you do not *ask* God for it."[2]

James had learned the necessity of asking from Jesus Himself. As the band of twelve men traveled from village to village with the Master, how often they had watched Him compel a supplicant to state his request straight out in plain terms. The Master would tolerate no generalities, no fuzziness. Like the day in Jericho when two blind men kept calling after Jesus, repeating over and over, "O Lord, Son of David, have pity on us!" [3]

The beggars' blindness was as obvious to Jesus as to the disciples. Yet the Master had silenced the men's singsong chant with the blunt question, "What do you want me to do for you?"

The directness of the question shocked the beggars out of their self-pitying, pious stance. "Lord," they told Him with a new directness, "we want our eyes opened."

Instantly, Jesus responded. At such moments, it was the look of love and compassion on their Master's face that James and the others would remember afterwards. How poignantly He cared about people! So Jesus had touched the eyes of each beggar in turn, and immediately their eyes received sight.

After watching a procession of such incidents, gradually the disciples came to know this as Jesus' way. . . . "Tell Me exactly what you want," He was always saying. "Talk to Me. *Ask* Me."

The importance of expressing our needs to our heavenly Father was a point He came back to over and over in His teaching:

. . . how much more will your Father in heaven give good gifts to those who *ask* him? [4]

Ask and the gift will be yours . . . for everyone who *asks* receives . . . . [5]

. . . *ask* and you will receive, that your joy may be full. [6]

He went on to teach that when we ask for bread, we won't get a stone. If we ask for an egg, God won't give us a scorpion any more than an earthly father would. [7] When we knock on the door, the door will swing open before us. Thus daringly, Jesus insisted that the answer to prayer is receiving what we ask for.

As the disciples listened to such statements, did blunt Peter or skeptical Thomas ever blurt out to their Master the question we often wonder about, "But Lord, since the Father in heaven knows everything about us and our needs anyway, what's the point of having to ask?"

Jesus' answer to this is implicit in much of His teaching about prayer. He had a great deal to say about the connection between prayer and childlikeness:

> . . . anyone who refuses to come to God as a little child will never be allowed into his Kingdom.[8]

How often Jesus prefaced some teaching to His big, burly disciples with an affectionate: "Little children, I tell you . . . ." And of course, the characteristic position of childhood is that of simple asking.

A little child who has no shyness or hesitation about asking his parents for what he needs is unselfconsciously revealing his helplessness—along with a normal, right relationship with his father and mother. In the same way, asking immediately puts us into a right relationship to God. It is acting out the fact that He is the Creator with the riches and resources we need; we are the creatures who need help. It's a cap-in-hand stance which we resist because it diminishes us—a certain amount of pride and self has to go for us to ask for help—whether of God or of another human being.

Simple happenings uncover our pride and stubbornness about asking—like the motorist who loses his way. Often we will go miles off our route, waste time trying one road after another, rather than stop to ask for the help we need.

God insists that we ask, not because *He* needs to know our

situation, but because *we* need the spiritual discipline of asking. Similarly, making our requests specific forces us to take a step forward in faith. The reason many of us retreat into vague generalities when we pray is not because we think too highly of God, but because we think too little. If we pray for something definite and our request is not granted, we fear to lose the little faith we had. So we fall back on the safe route of highly "spiritual" prayers—the kind that Jesus brushed aside as not true prayer at all, just self-deceptive "talking to ourselves." [9]

In commenting on such non-prayers in his famous book *The Screwtape Letters,* C. S. Lewis has the devil, Screwtape, give this advice to his understudy, Wormwood:

> It is, no doubt, impossible to prevent his praying for his mother, but we have means of rendering the prayers in-nocuous. Make sure that they are very "spiritual," that he is always concerned with the state of her soul and never with her rheumatism. . . .[10]

Oddly, we who are afraid to ask that the pain of rheumatism be removed or a lost contact lens found, often do not hesitate to pray for world peace or the salvation of souls or a revival to change the face of our time. It never occurs to us that if God's power is lacking for these everyday prayers, His power to handle big, all-inclusive petitions will be lacking too.

In order to make sure that we are not retreating from the tension of faith, it is helpful to ask ourselves as we pray, "Do I really expect anything to happen?" This will prevent us from going window-shopping in prayer. At times window-shopping can be enjoyable—but there it ends. It costs nothing. We are just looking, have no intention of buying anything; so we bring nothing home to show for the hours of browsing. Too many of our prayers—private and public—are just browsing amongst possible petitions, not down to cases at all. We expect nothing from our prayers except perhaps a euphoric feeling.

As for our losing faith in God if our request is not granted in the precise form we wish, can any of us possibly be as concerned about the state of our faith as God is? That we should trust Him is not only His will, but the passion of His Father-heart. Surely then, we can turn over to His keeping any worry about our losing faith.

Beyond that, are we afraid that a *no* answer will back us up against our own deficiencies, our failure to meet God's conditions? And if so, again, are we not really questioning God's ability to supply *everything* we lack—faith or perseverance or inner tensile strength to meet His conditions?

Jesus spoke often of heaven's "rewards." If that offends us by seeming too materialistic, perhaps we should be wary of being more "spiritual" than our Lord.

One veteran prayer warrior, John R. Rice, has expressed it bluntly in *Asking and Receiving:* "Prayer is not a lovely sedan for a sight-seeing trip around the city. Prayer is a truck that goes straight to the warehouse, backs up, loads, and comes home with the goods. . . ." [11]

If we think we'll never be able to summon the faith for such prayer, we're right. However, those saints who have had the most experience here tell us that God uses our most stumbling, faltering faith-step as the open door to His doing for us "more than we ask or think." We decide to ask His help with some small immediate need. Our asking is like stepping into a tiny anteroom. Taking a hesitant step forward, we discover that the anteroom leads into the King's spacious reception hall. To our astonishment, the King Himself comes forward to meet us, offering a gift so momentous as to be worthy only of the King: a lifetime gift of a friendship with the Lord of Glory.

"You asked Me for money for this month's rent," He smiles. "Sit here at My feet and we'll talk about the rent, but also of other matters too. I have much to say to you. If you accept My friendship, you and I have years of joyous interchange ahead. I've so much to teach you. It's going to take eternity to handle all of it."

Our situation reminds us of that nameless woman long ago, of whom the Master asked a drink of water from Jacob's Well at Sychar. Under the Stranger's penetrating gaze and His incisive questions, she found that the thirst that necessitated her daily trip to the well was but her surface problem. The Rabbi knew all about her, all the rotten things she'd ever done. Yet there was no condemnation, just a tender, healing love pointing her to the answers she had sought so long.[12]

Even so, our entering into a one-to-One relationship with Jesus enables Him to handle not only our immediate material and physical needs, but also deeper needs, the hidden ones involving right attitudes and healthy emotions, proper motivation, and how to solve our relationship problems.

Soon we discern that asking involves more than verbalization. Our lips do not always communicate accurately the heart's true cry. In some instances, that's because we are so out of touch with our own emotions that our prayers deal in unrealities. Sometimes we are divided within ourselves about what we actually want, so that we cannot ask wholeheartedly. Or perhaps we do not even know enough about our hopes and dreams to make our asking specific.

Then, we conclude, there must be different levels of asking. There's so much I want to learn about that: "Lord, teach me to pray."

I DO ASK

Lord Jesus, You who were born in a stable and laid in the straw, You who walked dusty roads and were thirsty, and relished the feel of cool water sliding down Your throat, and laughed, and sometimes cried salty tears—You are the One summoning me back to reality. I see it now—what I have considered lofty spirituality is sham and humbug in Your eyes. Worse than that, often it has been a cloak to hide my fear of not receiving what I ask You for.

You who are so much more alive than I am, now want to go with me down the city street and help me find a parking place, and remind me where I misplaced that slip of paper with the telephone number. You want to give my wife a good night's sleep, to heal my neighbor's arthritis, to help John find a job. Happiness floods my heart at the knowledge of Your being *Man* as well as God; the essence of any difficulty I ever encounter, You have experienced before me.

So You are bidding me tell You my every need and promising that joy and good gifts await my asking. Lord, I sorely need _____. I would also ask You for _____.

Would You give me Your thoughts about these requests? Is it, without my suspecting it, a petition for harm and not for good? Is there some step of growth, forgiveness, obedience that I must take before You can grant my request? And Lord, if I need patience to wait out Your perfect timing, then I also ask You to supply the patience.

In joyful anticipation, I await Your answer. Thank You, Lord Jesus. *Amen.*

CHAPTER TWO

THE PRAYER OF HELPLESSNESS

When I lived in the nation's capital, I used to notice how often the Washington papers reported suicide leaps from the Calvert Street Bridge. In fact, this happens so repeatedly that the site is often called "suicide bridge."

Sensing the human drama behind these brief notices—like the plunge of the Air Corps major's thirty-one-year-old wife with inoperable cancer, or that of the elderly man whose wife had just died—I often thought that there was probably a common denominator in all of these tragedies. Each person must have felt helpless. And I have thought, "If I could speak with such persons at the zero hour, I would try to stop them with the thought that helplessness is one of the greatest assets a human being can have."

For I believe that the old cliché, "God helps those who help themselves," is not only misleading but often dead wrong. My

most spectacular answers to prayers have come when I was so
helpless, so out of control as to be able to do nothing at all for
myself.

The Psalmist says: *When I was hemmed in, thou hast freed
me often.*[1] Gradually I have learned to recognize this hem-
ming-in as one of God's most loving devices for teaching us
that He is real and gloriously adequate for our problems.

One such experience occurred during the writing of my first
book. As the young widow of Peter Marshall, Scottish Presbyterian pastor and Chaplain of the United States Senate, I was
attempting what many felt was the rather audacious project of
writing his biography. About midway in the manuscript, I received devastating criticism from one whose judgment I trusted.
He told me bluntly, "You haven't even begun to get inside the
man Peter Marshall." And he was right, that was the sting of it.
The realization of my inadequacy as a writer was not only an
intellectual one. It was also emotional; there were plenty of
tears. But out of the crisis came a major realization.

In my helplessness, there was no alternative but to put the
project into God's hands. I prayed that *A Man Called Peter* be
His book, and that the results be all His too.

And they were. I still regard as incredible the several million
copies of *A Man Called Peter* circulating around the world. But
that and the successful 20th Century-Fox motion picture were
of little importance compared to what I hear from time to time
of lives changed through this book—of men entering the ministry through the inspiration of Peter Marshall's life.

Years later I saw the Prayer of Helplessness work in an
everyday situation—the matter of household help. Before my
marriage to Leonard LeSourd in the fall of 1959, I was full of
trepidation at the thought of taking on the care of his three
young children. My son, Peter John, had been away at school

for over three years, and I had involved myself with a writing career. In his efforts to reassure me, Len was blithe with promises of household help.

But the help situation in Chappaqua, New York proved unbelievably tight. Months passed. One woman stayed a few weeks, then left. We tried the classified columns without success; persistent prayer brought us no nearer a solution. I finally decided I would have to do it all myself, but soon found it was more than a full-time job running a lively household: week after week I did not get near my desk.

So—once again the old familiar pattern—the Prayer of Helplessness—the admission that I could not do everything myself—then the insight that my main responsibility was to our home. If God wanted me to resume my writing, He would show me the way.

After that admission of helplessness, Lucy Arsenault was sent to us. Lucy—steady, reliable, loyal, a marvelous cook, a great person.

Why would God insist on helplessness as a prerequisite to answered prayer? One obvious reason is because our human helplessness is bedrock fact. God is a realist and insists that we be realists too. So long as we are deluding ourselves that human resources can supply our heart's desires, we are believing a lie. And it is impossible for prayers to be answered out of a foundation of self-deception and untruth.

Then what is the truth about our human condition? None of us had anything to do with our being born; no control over whether we are male or female, Japanese or Russian or American, white or yellow or black. Nor can we influence our ancestry, nor our basic mental or physical equipment.

After we are born, an autonomic nervous system controls every vital function that sustains life. A power that no one really understands keeps our heart beating, our lungs breathing, our blood circulating, our body temperature at 98.6 degrees.

A surgeon can cut tissues, but he is helpless to force the body to bind the severed tissue together again.

We grow old relentlessly and automatically.

Self-sufficient? Scarcely!

Even the planet on which we live . . . we had nothing to do with its creation either. The little planet Earth is exactly the right distance—some ninety-three million miles—from the source of its heat and light. Any nearer and we would be consumed by solar radiation; any farther and we would be frozen to death. The balance of oxygen and nitrogen in the air is exactly right for the support of life, the elements in our soil, and the creation of rare rock deposits—all of this goes on quite apart from man—little man who struts and fumes upon the earth.

Did Jesus have any comment to make about all this? Yes, as always, He put His finger on the very heart of the matter: ". . . without me ye can do nothing," He said.[2]

Nothing? That seems a trifle sweeping. After all, we men have made great progress. We've almost eliminated diseases like smallpox, bubonic plague, tuberculosis, polio, and most of the communicable diseases of childhood. We have learned to control our environment to quite an extent. We have put men on the moon. How can all that be helplessness? Most of us do not enjoy that idea. The cult of humanism in our day has trained us to believe that we are quite adequate to be masters of our own destiny.

Yet not only did Jesus insist on the truth of our helplessness; He underscored it by telling us that this same helplessness applied equally to Him while He wore human flesh: "I can of mine own self do nothing: [He told His apostles,] The Father in me doeth the works." [3] In this as in everything else, He was setting the pattern of perfect humanity.

The Scriptures spell out for us point by point how helpless we are in relation to our spiritual lives as well as our physical ones. . . .

We feel an impulse towards God. *We* think that *we* are reaching out for Him. Not so, Jesus told us, "No one is able to come to me unless he is drawn by the Father . . . ." [4]

We want salvation from our sins, and eternal life. We think that we can earn this salvation. No. The truth is ". . . it is the gift of God: Not of works, lest any man should boast." [5]

So far as the virtues and graces we need for victory in our lives—faith, joy, patience, peace of mind, the ability to love the wretched and the unlovely—there is no way we can work up such qualities. Paul tells us in Galatians 5:22, 23 that these are gifts of the Holy Spirit. They can be had in no other way. ". . . A man can receive nothing, except it be given him from heaven." [6]

This emphasis on our helplessness is found over and over in the writings of Christians in other eras. For instance, in that little jewel of a seventeenth-century book, Brother Lawrence's *The Practice of the Presence of God,* helplessness was the hinge upon which turned the Carmelite lay brother's relationship with God:

> That when an occasion of practising some virtue offered, he addressed himself to God, saying, LORD, *I cannot do this unless Thou enablest me;* and that then he received strength more than sufficient.

> That when he had failed in his duty, he only confessed his fault, saying to GOD, *I shall never do otherwise if You leave me to myself; it is You who must hinder my falling, and mend what is amiss.* That after this he gave himself no further uneasiness about it. [7]

Though few of us have Brother Lawrence's maturity, never-theless, sometime in life every one of us finds himself out of control, caught in circumstances that he is helpless to change. When this happens, welcome such times! Often it is only then that we lesser spirits enter into the truth of Jesus' statement from the fifteenth chapter of John: "Apart from Me ye can do nothing."

Dr. Arthur Gossip, who wrote the exposition on John for the *Interpreter's Bible,* has this interesting comment: "These are surely the most hopeful words in Scripture . . . *Apart from Me ye can do nothing.* For it is on the basis of that frank recog-nition of our utter fecklessness apart from Him, that Christ . . . gives us His great promises . . . ."

Great promises, like that glorious one, sweeping enough to make up a thousand times over for our helplessness: ". . . with God all things are possible." [8] He is telling us that an omnip-otent, transcendent, and imminent God is above all and through all far more completely than we realize.

With helplessness alone, one would be like a bird trying to fly with one wing. But when the other wing of God's adequacy is added to our helplessness, then the bird can soar triumphantly above and through problems that hitherto have defeated us.

I have always been impressed by the story of Dr. A. B. Simp-son, a famous New York preacher.[9] Poor health had haunted this man. Two nervous breakdowns plus a heart condition led a well-known New York physician to tell him when he was only thirty-eight that he would never live to be forty.

The physician's diagnosis only underscored the physical help-lessness that the minister knew only too well. Preaching was an agonizing effort. Climbing even a slight elevation brought on a suffocating agony of breathlessness.

In desperation, sick in body and despairing in spirit, at last

Dr. Simpson went to his Bible to find out exactly what Jesus had to say about disease. He became convinced that He had always meant healing to be a part of His Gospel for the redemption of man's total being.

One Friday afternoon soon after this revelation, Dr. Simpson took a walk in the country. He was forced to walk painfully, slowly, for he was always out of breath. Coming to a pine woods, he sat down on a log to rest. Soon he found himself praying, telling God of his complete helplessness with regard to his physical condition. But to this helplessness he added his belief that God was "for health" all the way. It was that majestically powerful combination again, "My total inadequacy—Your perfect adequacy." He then asked Christ to enter him and to become his physical life for all the needs of his body until his lifework was done.

"There in the woods, I made a connection with God," he said later. "Every fiber in me was tingling with the sense of God's presence."

A few days after that, Simpson climbed a mountain three thousand feet high. "When I reached the top," he related joyfully, "the world of weakness and fear was lying at my feet. From that time on I had literally a new heart in my breast."

And so he did. During the first three years after this healing he preached more than a thousand sermons; sometimes as many as twenty meetings in one week. His testimony was that never once did he feel exhausted. For the rest of his life, he was noted for the amazing volume of his sermonic, pastoral, and literary work. He lived to be seventy-six.

Moreover, Simpson's work has lived after him. The Christian and Missionary Alliance which he founded is still a potent spiritual force today; his books are still being published and have blessed millions.

Why is prayer so startlingly effective when we admit our helplessness? First, as we have seen, because God insists upon our facing up to the true facts of our human situation. Thus we lay under our prayer-structure the firm foundation of truth rather than self-delusion or wishful thinking.

This recognition and acknowledgment of our helplessness is also the quickest way to that right attitude which God recognizes as essential to prayer. It deals a mortal blow to the most serious sin of all—man's independence that ignores God.

Another reason is that we cannot learn firsthand about God— what He is like, His love for us as individuals, and His real power—so long as we are relying on ourselves and other people. And fellowship with Jesus is the true purpose of life and the only foundation for eternity. It is real, this daily fellowship He offers us.

So if your every human plan and calculation has miscarried, if, one by one, human props have been knocked out, and doors have shut in your face, take heart. God is trying to get a message through to you, and the message is: "Stop depending on inadequate human resources. Let Me handle the matter."

Here are three suggestions for presenting to Him the Prayer of Helplessness.

First, be honest with God. Tell Him that you are aware of the fact that in His eyes you are helpless. Give God permission to make you feel your helplessness *at the emotional level,* if that's what He wants. And recognize that this may be painful. There is good psychological reason why this first step is necessary. Unless the power of our emotions is touched, it is as if a fuse remains unlit.

Second, take your heart's desire to God. You have accepted your helplessness. Now grip with equal strength of will your belief that God can do through you what you cannot. It may seem to you for a time that you are relying on emptiness, dangling over a chasm. Disregard these feelings, and quietly thank God that He is working things out.

Third, watch now for opening doors. When the right door opens, you will have a quiet inner assurance that God's hand is on the knob. That is the time of action for you, an opportunity for creativity.

One sunny day in the future, you will look back and your heart will overflow with praise to God that He cared about you enough to shut you up to Him alone. Without that stringently kind providence you could never have learned firsthand the amazing power of the Prayer of Helplessness.

WHERE ARE YOU, LORD?

Lord, I have been so defeated by circumstances. I have felt like an animal trapped in a corner with nowhere to flee. Where are *You* in all this, Lord? The night is dark. I cannot feel Your presence.

Help me to know that the darkness is really "Shade of Your hand, outstretched caressingly;" [10] that the "hemming in" is Your doing. Perhaps there was no other way You could get my full attention, no other way I would allow You to demonstrate what You can do in my life.

I see now that the emptier my cup is, the more space there is to receive Your love and supply. Lord, I hand to You this situation: _____, asking You to fill it from Your bountiful reservoirs in Your own time and Your own way.

How I thank You, Father in heaven, that Your riches are available to me, not on the basis of my deserving, but of Jesus and His worthiness. Therefore, in the strength of His name, I pray. *Amen.*

CHAPTER THREE

THE PRAYER THAT HELPS YOUR DREAMS COME TRUE

One of the most provocative facts I know is that every man-made object, as well as most activity in your life and mine, starts with an idea or a picture in the mind. My mother first taught me this, and at the same time she vividly demonstrated to me the prayer that helps dreams come true.

In my teens I long had the dream of going to college. But this was a depression time and the West Virginia church my father served was suffering financially too. I was accepted at Agnes Scott College in Decatur, Georgia, had saved some money from debating prizes, had the promise of a work scholarship—yet we were still several hundred dollars short.

One evening Mother found me lying across my bed, face-down, sobbing. She sat down beside me. "You and I are going to pray about this," she said quietly. We went into the guest room and knelt beside the old-fashioned, golden oak bed, the one that Mother and Father had bought for their first home. "I know it's right for you to go to college," Mother said. "I believe

God planted this dream in you; let's ask Him to tell us how to bring it to reality."

During those quiet moments in the bedroom, confidence and fresh determination flowed in. Mother's faith was contagious. The answer would come. How, we did not know.

I went ahead and made preparations for Agnes Scott. A short time later, Mother received an offer from the Federal Writers' Project to write the history of the county. Her salary was enough to pay for the major part of my college expenses.

An even more dramatic example of Mother's use of this Dreaming Prayer involved a young man from "Radical Hill," a run-down section of our West Virginia town. Raymond Thomas, who lived with foster parents, had no idea who his real parents were.

Dressed in working clothes and knee-high clodhoppers, Ray used to come to talk with my mother. He was always clean, but he didn't even own a suit of clothes. Of a summer's day he would settle himself on the top step of our vine-shaded front porch talking . . . talking . . . while Mother sat in a wooden rocker shelling peas or stringing beans or darning socks. Mother soon saw his boundless energy and fine mind.

On one particular afternoon there emerged for Ray the same inner longing which I had had—college. Once his dream was out in the open, standing there shimmering, poised in the air, Mother was delighted to see the wistfulness in Ray's brown eyes replaced by kindling hope.

"But how can I manage it?" the boy asked. "I've no money saved. Nor any prospects."

Mother sensed that with Ray, however, the Dreaming Prayer should involve, more than just college, a completely new approach to life. "Raymond, whatever you need, God has the supply ready for you, provided you're ready to receive it. And ours is still a land of opportunity, Raymond. The sky is the limit! The money will be there for every dream that's right for you, every dream for which you're willing to work."

For a preacher's wife who had little enough herself, this was a doughty philosophy. But Mother believed it and had often proved it so. And these truths took root in Ray.

There came the day when Ray accepted Mother's philosophy so completely that she could lead him in the prayer that releases dreams to make them come true. After having heard her pray it for me, I can easily imagine how it was for Ray . . . .

"Father, You've given Raymond a fine mind. We believe You want that mind to be developed, that You want Raymond's potential to be used to help You lift and lighten some portion of Your world. Since all the wealth of the world is Yours, please help Raymond find everything he needs for an education.

"And, Father, we also believe you have even bigger plans for Raymond. Plant in his mind and heart the vivid pictures, the specific dreams that reflect Your plans for him after college. And oh, give him joy in dreaming—great joy."

With a flat pocketbook but faith in his dream, Raymond Thomas got on a bus and went off to college. How he made it is much too long to chronicle here. It involved Mother's finding a woman to start him off with a loan—writing him encouraging letters—praying. And Ray himself accepting responsibility, developing initiative. In four years he had twelve jobs, budgeting time as well as money: so many hours for classes, study, church work, recreation. It was a proud day for Mother when Ray received his Bachelor of Science degree, *cum laude.*

During World War II and afterwards I lost touch with Ray, though I knew he had settled in Vienna. Then in the summer of 1958, I wrote Ray that I was coming to Europe.

In Rome I found a letter from him waiting for me . . . .

I have a surprise for you. You will hear from the office of the Reveranda Fabrica di San Pietro whom I've contacted on your behalf. The point is that only with their permission can you see the most wonderful sight in Rome, the excavated street of tombs sixteen centuries old beneath the nave of the High Altar in St. Peter's. I explored every bit of it two years ago . . . .

Then when I checked into the hotel in Florence, the mail clerk handed me another letter from Ray . . . .

When you see the high dome of the Duomo, remember that it took Brunelleschi fourteen years to build it. Last winter I climbed to the highest balcony right at the top of the dome and crawled all around it . . . .

By now I was consumed with curiosity about Ray. This man seemed to bear no resemblance to the boy from Radical Hill. Obviously he knew Europe as few Americans do. And the drive and indefatigable zest apparent in his letters intrigued me.

The letters kept coming . . . Venice:

I've written to my friend at the Salviati Glass Works and asked him to send a gondola for you. You must see the master glassblowers at work . . . .

Bad Gastein:

You'll find it rugged. I've skied near there . . . .

Ray met me at the Vienna airport, a bouquet of flowers in hand. "Flowers and music are a part of Vienna," he explained. "Here we always take flowers to our hostess even for a dinner party." Later, over *Sacher torte* and coffee, he began answering my questions. "The fact that I could sit on your front steps and —with no money at all—dream of going to college and achieve it, proved something to me. Very simply, what your mother had said, was true—any right dream can be realized. Material resources *are* at the beck and call of the dreamer. And prayer helps you know if it is right and gives you the power to stay with it."

He described his war experience—one of the few survivors of a torpedoed destroyer—and how during convalescence he dreamed of the plan for the rest of his life.

"I wanted to be the kind of world citizen who could serve my country in peacetime, to travel and master several languages, to get a Ph.D. degree."

"It interests me that your dreams were that specific," I interposed.

Ray sipped his coffee, seeming lost in thought as he stared out of the window. "This dreaming process won't work unless we *are* specific. That's because a big part of the power to make the dream come true arises from a mental picture. And you sure do have to have specifics to form a mental picture."

Then Ray went on to sum up how much of his dream had been realized: travel in sixty countries, his Ph.D. in physics from the University of Vienna, which meant mastering German. He also speaks Spanish, passable French, some Italian, Dutch and Swedish—and a little Russian. He serves his country through a job with the U.S. Atomic Energy Program in Europe.

A story like Ray's reveals the connection between constructive dreaming and prayer. For, in a sense all such dreaming is praying. It is certainly the Creator's will that the desires and talents that He Himself has planted in us be realized. God is supremely concerned about the fulfillment of the great person He envisions each of us. He wants us to catch from Him some of

His vision for us. After all, this is what prayer is, men cooperating with God in bringing from heaven to earth His wondrously good plans for us.

Sadly, sometimes we fail to catch His vision for us because our capacity to dream has been atrophied by some condition which has given us a poverty-complex. My first glimpse of this was in a former college friend who had suffered a poverty-stricken childhood. Dot, as I'll call her, was unable to visualize what she wanted in the vocational field.

Yet she had come to Washington with idealistic ideas about a government job. "I don't want just any job," Dot had explained to me soon after she arrived. "I go along with the idea that God has a plan for my life. Only I haven't yet found it, so how do I pray about this job situation?"

"What job would give you the most joy?" I asked her. "Usually that's a key to what one *should* do."

My friend merely looked puzzled and shook her head.

"Do you ever daydream?" I persisted. "Is there anything you've always longed to do?"

"No—o. Nothing."

The reason that this particular girl could not dream constructively was that during financially difficult years her widowed mother had taught her that those who hope for little or nothing will never suffer disappointment. Actually this had been nothing less than excellent training in poverty expectation. Sadly, I watched my friend fall into a routine government filing job that used but a fraction of her abilities.

I know now that there is healing for such a situation. When we become aware of such damaged areas in the unconscious, we can call on the power of the Holy Spirit. He can walk back with us into the past and drain out all poison, make the rough places smooth, and create a highway for our God to come marching triumphantly into the present with His long-forgotten, oft-delayed plan for our lives.

In fact, there is no limit to what this combination of dreams and prayer can achieve. I have seen amazing results in many areas: like finding the right mate or the right job, or locating the ideal house, or in rearing children, or in building a business.

The story of the Olivettis came to my attention some years ago when I visited their beautiful typewriter-and-office-equipment plant in Ivrea, northwest Italy in the Alps-ringed Canavese region. There I saw fifty-four carefully landscaped acres; nearby an infirmary for the workers; an employees' library; rows of pastel-colored apartments. The factory is as noted for its workers' benefits and enlightened welfare program as for its international success. And I was entranced to find that all of it is the result of a dream . . . .

One autumn day years ago a young Italian visitor stood in the yard of the Underwood factory in Hartford, Connecticut, staring at the red brick buildings. A passerby, seeing the young man, would have marveled at his total absorption, for there was nothing unusual about the rambling red brick buildings on which he was so intent: they looked like thousands of other New England factories.

Yet to Adriano Olivetti the old buildings represented a lifetime dream. At that time UNDERWOOD was the greatest name in typewriters. Someday, he vowed, he would own a company like that, and the name OLIVETTI would carry the same implication of quality. By fixing the actual physical buildings in his mind and heart, he was creating a mental image on which he could focus his prayers.

Thirty-four years later, Adriano returned to the United States as president of Ing. C. Olivetti & Co. At that time he telephoned a colleague in Italy to tell him the good news. "I have just bought something . . . ." Here his voice broke with emotion. "I've just bought the Underwood Company."

Eight million, seven hundred thousand dollars had just exchanged hands. With his acquisition of the control of the old American company, Adriano Olivetti had seen the fulfillment of his thirty-four-year-old dream.

There are those who are wary of this Prayer That Helps Your Dreams Come True because they are dubious about praying for material needs such as bread, clothing, a catch of fish, or to put it in modern terms, a parking place for a car. Rightly, they also ask, "Isn't there danger of trying to use God and spiritual principles for selfish ends?"

Each is a valid question that needs to be answered. As for whether God means for us to include material needs in our petitions, certainly Christ was interested in men's bodies as well as their souls. He was concerned about their diseases, their physical hunger. Christianity, almost alone among world religions, acknowledges material things as real and important—real enough that Christ had to die in a real body on a real Cross.

And as for the danger that our dreams may spring from our selfish human will rather than God's will, there are tests for this. Only when a dream has passed such a series of tests—so that we are certain that our heart's desire is also God's dream *before* we pray—can we pray the Dreaming Prayer with faith and thus with power.

Let's begin by acknowledging that God's laws are in operation in our universe—whether we recognize them or not. We have to cooperate with these laws, not defy them. For example, ask yourself questions like these:

- Will my dream fulfill the talents, the temperament, and emotional needs which God has planted in my being?

This is not easy to answer. It involves knowing oneself, the real person, as few of us do.

- Does my dream involve taking anything or any person belonging to someone else? Would its fulfillment hurt any other human being? If so, you can be fairly sure that this particular dream is not God's will for you.

- Am I willing to make all my relationships with other people right? If I hold resentments, grudges, bitterness —no matter how justified—these wrong emotions will cut me off from God, the source of creativity. Furthermore, no dream can be achieved in a vacuum of human relationships. Even one such wrong relationship can cut the channel of power.

- Do I want this dream with my whole heart? Dreams are not usually brought to fruition in divided personalities; only the whole heart will be willing to do its part toward implementing the dream.

- Am I willing to wait patiently for God's timing?

- Am I dreaming big? The bigger the dream and the more persons it will benefit, the more apt it is to stem from the infinite designs of God.

If your heart's desire can pass a series of tests like this, then you are ready for the final necessary step in the Dreaming Prayer! Hand your dream over to God, and then leave it in His keeping. There seem to be periods when the dream is like a seed that must be planted in the dark earth and left there to germinate. This is not a time of passiveness on our part. There are things we can and must do—fertilizing, watering, weeding— hard work and self-discipline.

But the growth of that seed, the mysterious and irresistible burgeoning of life in dark and in secret, *that* is God's part of the process. We must not keep digging up our dream, examining and measuring it to see how it is coming along. I will have more to say about the power of trustful and prayerful waiting in the following chapter.

But in the meantime, long before we see the fruition of our hopes, in fact the very moment a God-given dream is planted in our hearts, a strange happiness flows into us. I have come to think that at that moment all the resources of the universe are released to help us. Our praying is then at one with the will of God, a channel for the Creator's always joyous, triumphant purposes for us and our world.

GIVE ME A DREAM

Father, once—it seems long ago now—I had such big dreams, so much anticipation of the future. Now no shimmering horizon beckons me; my days are lackluster. I see so little of lasting value in the daily round. Where is Your plan for my life, Father?

You have told us that without vision, we men perish.[1] So Father in heaven, knowing that I can ask in confidence for what is Your expressed will to give me,[2] I ask You to deposit in my mind and heart the particular dream, the special vision You have for my life.

And along with the dream, will You give me whatever graces, patience, and stamina it takes to see the dream through to fruition? I sense that this may involve adventures I have not bargained for. But I want to trust You enough to follow even if You lead along new paths. I admit to liking some of my ruts. But I know that habit patterns that seem like cozy nests from the inside, from Your vantage point may be prison cells. Lord, if You have to break down any prisons of mine before I can see the stars and catch the vision, then Lord, begin the process now. In joyous expectation, *Amen*.

CHAPTER FOUR

THE WAITING PRAYER

One day not long ago I was flipping through a beloved, dog-eared old Bible that I had not used for a while when I came across a series of little egg-shaped slips of paper. I smiled, remembering what they were all about.

When my son Peter John was small and I was in a typical motherly mood of worrying about him, I came across a seemingly almost childlike piece of "how to" writing by Dr. Glenn Clark. Part of our problem in praying for our children, he suggested, is the time lag, the necessary slow maturation of our prayers. But that's the way of God's rhythm in nature. For instance, the hen must patiently sit on her eggs to incubate them before the baby chicks hatch.

With this picture in mind, Dr. Clark suggested that we parents spend some time each day for at least a week thinking through our hearts' deepest desires for our children. After listing them on paper, ask for Jesus' mind on them, sifting out everything superficial or selfish until we have reached the kernel of the Spirit's hopes and dreams for this particular person.

41

Then, said Dr. Clark, copy these hopes in the form of prayers onto slips of paper cut roughly into the shape of eggs. And then give these petitions to our Father to fulfill in His own time and His own way. To help dramatize the recognition that visible answers may be slow in coming, insert the slips of paper between the pages of some favorite Bible—signifying leaving them in God's keeping.

At the time I followed these suggestions, I did not mention to anyone what I had done for fear of seeming naive. Yet, today I think just the opposite. I feel that those little paper eggs represent a very profound principle indeed. For when I came across them in my Bible, I found to my astonishment that a loving Father had fulfilled every single request.

Why? What was there about that form of prayer that He honored so dramatically? Certainly it wasn't that I had cut out pieces of paper in a particular shape, or that there was any power in the physical presence of the Bible. As I pondered this, it occurred to me that part of the secret lay in the waiting. Waiting itself, if practiced according to Biblical patterns, seems to be a strange but dynamic kind of communication between man and God.

Waiting certainly plays an enormous role in the unfolding story of God's relationship to man. It is God's oft-repeated way of teaching us that His power is real and that He can answer our prayers without interference and manipulation from us.

But we have such trouble getting *our* will, *our* time schedules out of the way. Much of the time we act like a child who brings a broken toy to his father to be mended.[1] The father gladly takes the toy and begins work. Then after a while, childlike impatience takes over. Why is it taking so long?

The child stands by, getting his hands in the father's way, offering a lot of meaningless advice and some rather silly criticism. Finally in desperation, he snatches the toy from the father's hands and walks off with it, saying rather bitterly that he hadn't really thought his father could fix it anyway. Perhaps it isn't even "his will" to mend toys.

On the other hand, whenever we are trustful enough to leave our "broken toy" with the Father, not only do we eventually get it back gloriously restored, but are also handed a surprising plus. We find for ourselves what the saints and mystics affirm, that during the dark waiting period when self-effort had ceased, a spurt of astonishing spiritual growth took place in us. Afterwards we have qualities like more patience, more love for the Lord and those around us, more ability to hear His voice, greater willingness to obey.

The divine Husbandman has been teaching us the lesson of the Life in the Vine. During that waiting period (what seemed like a dark night of the soul) we were learning the great secret of *abiding*. Abiding is the key to unlock heaven's treasures.[2]

Our human hang-up is thinking that spirituality is something we *do*. "Not so," says Jesus. "Rather it is My life in you." The branch does not have to stretch and strain to grow and produce fruit. The branch's part is simply to remain connected to the Vine, to abide there so that the life-giving sap can flow. Then only do we "bear much fruit."

Jesus also had a great deal to say about His Father's timing, the principle that there is a God-given sequence and rate of growth for everything in His Creation:

. . . first the blade, then the ear, after that the full corn in the ear.[3]

"The time is fulfilled, and the kingdom of God is at hand," [4] Jesus might say. Or when certain disciples were trying to get Him to act prematurely, "My time is not yet come . . . ." [5] Later as the shadows deepened around the Cross, "My time is at hand." [6] Always *His* timing. We force and try to hurry the divine schedule at our peril.

God does have His "fullness of time" for the answer to each prayer. It follows then that He alone knows the magnitude of the changes that have to be wrought in us before we can receive our hearts' desires. He alone knows the changes and interplay of external events that must take place before our prayer can be answered. That's why Jesus told us, "It is not for you to know the times or the seasons, which the Father hath put in his own power." [7]

Thus the Lord seems constantly to use waiting as a tool for bringing us the very best of His gifts. He made the children of Israel wait generations for their freedom from slavery in Egypt. Because of their stubborn disobedience, they had to wait forty years before they were ready to enter the Promised Land. Waiting was the keynote of the exile. The whole story of the Old Testament is the patient waiting for "the fullness of time" of the Saviour's birth. And after Jesus' Ascension, those gathered in the upper room had to wait a full ten days for the coming of the Holy Spirit.

No wonder some of God's promises are predicated upon our waiting trustingly for His timing:

The Lord is good unto them that wait for him . . . .[8]

Those that wait on the Lord shall possess the land.[9]

But they that wait upon the Lord shall renew their strength; they shall mount up with wings as eagles; they shall run, and not be weary; and they shall walk, and not faint.[10]

For since the world began no one has seen or heard of such a God as ours, who works for those who wait for him! [11]

And let us not be weary in well doing: for in due season we shall reap, if we faint not.[12]

Waiting seems to be a kind of acted-out prayer that is required more often and honored more often than I could understand until I saw what remarkable faith-muscles this act develops. For isn't it true that waiting demands patience, persistence, trust, expectancy—all the qualities we are continually beseeching God to give us?

I remember once being in a situation where the Lord told me to wait, to stand silently by, saying nothing, even though I thought I knew the answer to a problem. Even within this smaller scope, I was to wait on His timing, His invisible action in another human heart. It was an astounding experience in poised expectancy.

I had not seen Helen in nearly two years. Her telephone call was a shocker because she told me that her husband, Steve, was leaving her for a younger woman. She wanted to talk. "Please, Catherine, may I come and see you?"

"Helen, I have no qualifications as a marriage counselor," I said.

"But you will pray with me, won't you?"

Yes, that I could certainly do and said so, little realizing what a strange form that prayer was to take.

Now, as Helen stood in the doorway of our home in Boynton Beach, Florida, I looked at her with a sinking heart. She was carelessly dressed, her eyes dull and bloodshot from weeping. She was overweight and her blonde-red hair needed attention.

As we settled down on the sofa in our living room Helen launched into a story that had one recurring theme—throughout, she was constantly putting herself down. They had three children, but Steve had wanted more. Steve spent most of his home hours in front of TV, but then—she had never been much of a conversationalist. He hadn't taken her out in years, but she didn't mind much. Helen wasn't sure who the other woman was,

but doubtless it was someone more stimulating—and so on
and on.

As Helen talked on, I suddenly realized that I knew what the
problem was. Not that it took much insight: Helen had been
screaming the news to me from the moment she walked in. This
woman couldn't stand herself. And the minute this became clear,
I knew something else. I was to say nothing. The Lord spoke to
my heart crisply. I was to wait. I was to sit on this piece of insight until the Lord gave it to Helen Himself, in His own time
and in His own way. The self-control required of me was incredible, as for two hours Helen spelled out in a score of different ways what I already knew. But incredible also was the sense
of expectancy as I watched the Lord at work. He had brought
Helen here for the specific purpose of giving her time—time to
think coherently and connectedly about her problem. I was there
only to keep her thoughts on the track. Helen needed to reach
her understanding on her own, and He was giving me super-
natural supplies of patience (for me) while He led her there
ever so gently.

With this gift of grace, the two hours sped by as I found myself almost leaning forward in anticipation. The time was a blend
of talking, reading Scriptures, silence, and listening. At last
Helen asked me if she might go out into the garden to be alone
for a while.

When she returned, her words came tumbling out, "That
Bible verse, Catherine, about Jesus loving us before we loved
Him—recently it's been hard to believe that *anyone* loves me.
But out there in your garden I got to thinking. When you really
believe that God loves you as a person, well then you've got to
love yourself, too."

I nodded, not daring to speak, and she went on: "Well, it just
occurred to me that I've dishonored Him, in a sense, by the way

I let myself and the house get run-down. I mean my weight, TV dinners all the time, beds never made . . . ."

As I listened, I marveled at God's ways. If I had tried to say these things to Helen as a friend giving advice, chances are she would have taken offense, or at best accepted my suggestions reluctantly. Needless to say, this did not solve the problems in Helen's marriage overnight; there were many rough months to follow. But eventually, as Helen cleaned up her house and her person, swept out resentments and smothered angers, and came to see herself for the cherished person she was in God's eyes, the marriage too was healed. As I know from the amazing long-distance phone call that came from her over a year later. "I just thought you'd like to know, Catherine, that Steve and I are back together. We're off on a sort of second honeymoon now. We're spending hours just talking . . . ."

So the Bible extols waiting, partly because it requires qualities which the Lord wants to encourage in us, like patience, which I need so badly. But there is another reason too. Waiting works. It is a joining of man and God to achieve an end, and the end is always a form of the Easter story.

An incident I've never forgotten is related by Patt Barnes of Milwaukee, who tells of an aged flower vendor he once met who taught him the secret of the "three days." Patt Barnes was so impressed by the old woman's visible radiant joy that he commented that her life must be remarkably trouble free. Oh no, she said, she had as many troubles as the next one, but she knew that problems held a resurrection hidden within them. When Jesus died, all looked black, but then three days later came Easter. "So that's why I'm happy," she said. "I know the secret. When trouble comes, give God a chance—wait three days."

We can allow an apparent defeat to turn into victory through trusting in the principle of resurrection. The time may not be a literal three days, but the principle is always the same. Nor, as the Bible prototype (Easter) was not a passive event, neither is this kind of waiting. Here too, something must be put to death, usually worry or trying to "do it yourself."

Some years ago a friend of mine in Washington confided to me a kind of prayer she was saying for her son, then a boy of ten. "Already I've begun praying for that just-right marriage partner for Bobby. I pray for this future wife's protection from evil, for her proper growth, both physical and spiritual," she told me.

That was a new idea to me. But it struck me as so right that I acted on it. Each morning for some days, I worked on that creative type of prayer which, I had learned from experience, God delights to honor. I asked myself, "What would be the characteristics of spirit and mind and heart of that just-right girl for my son?" I was not so much concerned with whether she would be a blonde or a brunette; surely, the inner beauty would indicate the outer.

Item by item—quite specifically—the lineaments of my dream girl were put on paper. Most importantly, she would have met Jesus Christ for herself and would have fallen in love with Him. She would have a good mind, enough education for mutual intellectual stimulation. She would have a lot of the joy of life in her, a sense of humor, a certain zing—and so on.

Then when the portrait seemed complete, one morning I gave it to the Lord, asking Him to correct any flaws in it and bring it to fruition in Peter's life in His own time and His own way. I buried it, as it were, as a farmer buries his seed, by placing the notes about my dream girl between the pages of the same favorite Bible.

In the years that followed it was difficult not to dig the seed up again and examine it as in time, a procession of girls passed through Peter's life. Many were attractive; some would have been hard to accept. But the time of creative waiting came to an end when Peter John was in his middle year at Princeton Seminary. The girl's name was Edith.

Sometime after Edith and Peter were engaged I came across those written notes and reread them with amazement. There— detail by detail—was Edith. Of course, as always, God had thrown in a few extra goodies for dividends. She was tall, like Peter; blonde, like Peter; a wonderful cook—what man wouldn't like that? She was strong physically, with joyous vitality. And she was interested in gardening and handicrafts and other hobbies which Peter enjoys. I loved her immediately and have never stopped thanking God for such a marvelous answer to the mysterious, triumphant Waiting Prayer.

WHILE I WAIT

Lord Jesus, You want honest words on my lips: no thought of mine is hidden from You anyway . . . I am puzzled about the Father's timing. You know how long I have been praying about _____
_____, and I have tried to be patient about the answer. But Lord, why does Your providence have to move so slowly?

I know that the seasons come and go in majestic sequence. The earth rotates on its axis in a predetermined rhythm. No prayers of mine could change any of this. I know that Your ways are not my ways; Your timing is not my timing. But Lord, how do I, so earthbound, come to terms with the pace of eternity?

I want to be teachable, Lord. Is there something You want to show me, some block You want removed, some change You want in me or my attitudes before You can answer my prayer? Give me the gift of eyes that see, of ears that hear what You are saying to me.

Come Lord Jesus, and abide in my heart. How grateful I am to realize that the answer to my prayer does not depend on me at all. As I quietly abide in You and let Your life flow into me, what freedom it is to know that the Father does not see my threadbare patience or insufficient trust, rather only Your patience, Lord, and Your confidence that the Father has everything in hand.

In Your faith I thank You right now for a more glorious answer to my prayer than I can imagine. *Amen.*

CHAPTER FIVE

THE PRAYER OF RELINQUISHMENT

Like most people, when I first began active experimentation with prayer, I was full of questions, such as: Why are some agonizingly sincere prayers granted, while others are not?

Today I still have questions. Mysteries about prayer are always ahead of knowledge—luring, beckoning on to further experimentation.

But one thing I do know; I learned it through hard experience. It is a way of prayer that has resulted consistently in a glorious answer, glorious because each time power beyond human reckoning has been released. This is the Prayer of Relinquishment.

I got my first glimpse of it in the fall of 1943. I had then been ill for six months with a widespread lung infection, and a bevy of specialists seemed unable to help. Persistent prayer, using all the faith I could muster, had resulted in—nothing. I was still in bed full time.

One afternoon a pamphlet was put in my hands. It was the story of a missionary who had been an invalid for eight years. Constantly she had prayed that God would make her well, so that she might do His work. Finally, worn out with futile petition, she prayed, "All right. I give up. If You want me to be an invalid, that's Your business. Anyway, I want You even more than I want health. You decide." In two weeks the woman was out of bed, completely well.

This made no sense to me, yet I could not forget the story. On the morning of September 14—how can I ever forget the date?—I came to the same point of abject acceptance. "I'm tired of asking," was the burden of my prayer. "I'm beaten, finished. God, You decide what You want for me."

Tears flowed. I felt no faith as I understood faith, expected nothing. The gift of my sick self was made with no trace of graciousness.

And the result? It was as if I had touched a button that opened windows in heaven; as if some dynamo of heavenly power began flowing, flowing. Within a few hours I had experienced the presence of the Living Christ in a way that wiped away all doubt and revolutionized my life. From that moment my recovery began.

Through this incident and others that followed, God was trying to teach me something important about prayer. Gradually, I saw that a demanding spirit, with self-will as its rudder, blocks prayer. I understood that the reason for this is that God absolutely refuses to violate our free will; that therefore, unless self-will is voluntarily given up, even God cannot move to answer prayer.

In time, I gained more understanding about the Prayer of Relinquishment through the experiences of others, both in contemporary life and through books. Jesus' prayer in the Garden

of Gethsemane, I came to see, is the pattern for us. Christ could
have avoided the Cross. He did not have to go up to Jerusalem
the last time. He could have compromised with the priests,
bargained with Caiaphas. He could have capitalized on His following and appeased Judas by setting up the beginning of an
earthly Kingdom. Pilate wanted to release Him, all but begged
Him to say the right words that would let him do so. Even in
the Garden on the night of the betrayal, He had plenty of time
and opportunity to flee. Instead Christ used His free will to
turn the decision over to His Father.

The Phillips translation of the Gospels brings Jesus' prayer
into special focus: "Dear Father . . . all things are possible
to you. Let me not have to drink this cup! Yet it is not what I
want but what you want." [1]

The prayer was not answered as the human Jesus wished.
Yet power has been flowing from His Cross ever since.

Even at the moment when Christ was bowing to the possibility
of an awful death by crucifixion, He never forgot either the
presence or the power of God. There is a crucial difference here
between acceptance and resignation. There is no resignation in
the Prayer of Relinquishment. Resignation says, "This is my
situation, and I resign myself and settle down to it." Resignation
lies down in the dust of a godless universe and steels itself for
the worst.

Acceptance says, "True, this is my situation at the moment.
I'll look unblinkingly at the reality of it. But I'll also open my
hands to accept willingly whatever a loving Father sends."
Thus acceptance never slams the door on hope.

Yet even while it hopes, our relinquishment must be the real
thing—and this giving up of self-will is the hardest thing we
human beings are ever called on to do.

I remember the agony of one attractive young girl, Sara B.,

who shared with me her doubts about her engagement. "I love Jeb," she said, "and Jeb loves me. But the problem is, he drinks. Not that he's an alcoholic or anything. But the drinking is a sort of symbol of a lot of ideas he has. It keeps bothering me—enough that I wonder if God is trying to tell me to give up Jeb."

As we talked, Sara came to her own conclusion. It was that she would lose something infinitely precious if she did not follow the highest and the best that she knew. Tears glistened in her eyes as she said, "I'm going to break the engagement. If God wants me to marry Jeb, He will see that things change —about the drinking and all."

Right then, simply and poignantly, she told God of her decision. She was putting her broken dreams and her now unknown future into God's hands.

Jeb's ideas and ideals did not change, and Sara did not marry him. A year later Sara wrote me an ecstatic letter. "It nearly killed me to give up Jeb. Yet God knew that he wasn't the one for me. Recently I've met *the* man and we're to be married. Today I *really* have something to say about the wisdom and the joy of trusting God . . . ."

It's good to remember that not even the Master Shepherd can lead if the sheep do not follow Him but insist on running ahead of Him or taking side paths. That's the *why* of Christ's insistence on a very practical obedience: *And why call ye me, Lord, Lord, and do not the things which I say?* [2] Obey . . . obedience . . . trust . . . is all over the Gospels. The pliability of an obedient heart must be complete from the set of our wills right on through to our actions.

When we come right down to it, how can we make obedience real except as we give over our self-will in reference to each of life's episodes as it unfolds—whether we understand it or not, and even if evil appears to have initiated the episode in question? That's why it should not surprise us that at the heart of the secret of answered prayer lies the Law of Relinquishment.

So Mrs. Nathaniel Hawthorne, wife of the famous American author, found as she wrestled in prayer in the city of Rome one February day in 1860. Una, the Hawthorne's eldest daughter, was dying of a virulent form of malaria. The attending physician, Dr. Franco, had warned that afternoon that unless the young girl's fever abated before morning, she would die.

As Mrs. Hawthorne sat by Una's bed, her thoughts went to her husband in the adjoining room and what he had said earlier that day, "I cannot endure the alternations of hope and fear; therefore I have settled with myself not to hope at all."

But the mother could not share Nathaniel's hopelessness. Una could not, must not die. This daughter strongly resembled her father, had the finest mind, the most complex character of all the Hawthorne children. Why should some capricious Providence demand that they give her up?

Moreover, Una had been delirious for several days, had recognized no one. Were she to die this night, there could not even be the solace of farewells.

As the night deepened, the girl lay so still that she seemed to be in the anteroom of death. The mother went to the window and looked out on the piazza. There was no moonlight; a dark and silent sky was heavy with clouds.

"I cannot bear this loss—cannot—cannot . . . ." Then suddenly, unaccountably, another thought took over. "Why should I doubt the goodness of God? Let Him take Una, if He sees best. More than that: I can *give* her to Him! I do give her to You, Lord. I won't fight against You anymore."

Then an even stranger thing happened. Having made this great sacrifice, Mrs. Hawthorne expected to feel sadder. Instead

she felt lighter, happier than at any time since Una's long illness
had begun.

Some minutes later she walked back to the girl's bedside, felt
her daughter's forehead. It was moist and cool. Her pulse was
slow and regular. Una was sleeping naturally. And the mother
rushed into the next room to tell her husband that a miracle
had happened.

In the realm of answered prayer the progression of events in
Una's recovery was not unique. For in the years since I first
read the Hawthornes' story, I keep hearing of strikingly similar
experiences. This one was given me by a friend in a letter:

. . . . Three years ago our son was born. At first he seemed
a normal, healthy baby. But when he was not quite twelve
hours old, while I was holding him in my arms for the first
time, he had a convulsion. More convulsions followed in the
next few days.

The only explanation the doctors had was that he must have
suffered a brain injury of some kind at birth. This only
added to my terror. If he lived, perhaps he would be blind,
deaf, dumb, or a cripple, or with his mind affected.

I've never felt so alone during the time that followed. I
prayed, but I couldn't feel that God cared about me anymore. Why had this had to happen to *my* baby?

I know now that my prayers were not prayers at all, but
accusations. I was demanding that God heal my child.

Then out of sheer exhaustion of body and soul, I stopped
commanding God and gave in to Him completely. I just
said, "Take him if that's what You want. *Anything* You
decide will be all right with me. Even if You want him to
be crippled or retarded, then I will just have to learn to

accept it and live with it." I put myself entirely in His hands.

From that instant, not only did Larry begin to improve, but suddenly my tears left, and my fears went with them. An inexplicable peace filled my heart, and I knew, just knew that Larry would not only live but would have a normal, useful life. . . .

Well, the end of the story is that Larry is now a normal and healthy little boy. He's very, very intelligent, and if he were any more active, well, I'd be the one to be a cripple . . . .

It is obvious that Larry's story and Una's have several points in common. In each case, the mother wanted something desperately—life and health for her child. Each mother virtually commanded God to answer her prayer. While this demanding spirit had the upper hand, God seemed remote, unapproachable. Then through a combination of the obvious futility of the demanding prayer, plus weariness of body and spirit, the one praying surrendered to the possibility of what she feared most. At that instant, there came a turning point. Suddenly and unaccountably, fear left. Peace crept into the heart. There followed a feeling of lightness and joy that had nothing to do with outer circumstances. That was the turning point. From that moment, the prayer began to be answered.

Now the intriguing question is: What is the secret or spiritual law implicit in this Prayer of Relinquishment?

Here is part of it . . . . We know that fear is like a screen erected between us and God so that His power cannot get through to us. So, how does one get rid of fear?

This is not easy when the life of someone dear hangs in the balance, or when what we want most in all the world is involved.

At such times, every emotion, every passion, is tied up in the dread of what may happen. Obviously only drastic measures can deal with such a gigantic fear and the demanding spirit that usually goes along with it. My experience has been that trying to deal with it by repeating faith affirmations is not drastic enough.

So then we are squarely up against the Law of Relinquishment. Was Jesus showing us how to use this law when He said, "Resist not evil"? [3] Stop fleeing from and denying this terrible prospect. Look squarely at the possibility of what you fear most.

At the time, it seems to us that this is the opposite of trust. "Lord," we are inclined to protest, "didn't You tell us to pray with faith? I'm confused. Does relinquishment mean that we can never be sure about praying for any definite thing? If it does, Lord, then how can that be faith?"

To all such pleas to understand, Jesus always patiently gives the same answer, "Obey Me. Then—after that—you will know and begin to understand."

So we take the first hard steps of obedience. And lo, as we stop hiding our eyes, force ourselves to walk up to the fear and look it full in the face—never forgetting that God and His power are still the supreme reality—the fear evaporates. Drastic? Yes. But it is one sure way of releasing prayer power into human affairs.

Sometimes the miracle of prayer gloriously answered takes place at that point. With other situations the Good Shepherd leads us from relinquishment on into *knowing*. Such knowing is different from trying to think positively or making affirmations. It is not our doing at all; it is the gift of God. [4]

Sometimes the gift of faith is given to us through a verse of Scripture which leaps from the printed page or out of our remembrance and sets the heart afire. Or the knowing may come after a self-authenticating, interior Word from the Lord Himself about what is going to happen in our situation. Upon occasion, God may tell us that He cannot grant us what we have asked for, as in the case of Sara B. Obviously, we have not really meant business about the Prayer of Relinquishment until we have faced that eventuality too.

Whenever a loving Father grants our wish, the Word appears in exterior circumstances and the miracle happens—we understand that relinquishment and faith are not contradictory. The Prayer of Relinquishment is the child dropping his rebellion against being a child, placing his hand in the big, protective hand of the Father, and trusting Him to lead us even in the dark.

In the Prayer of Faith our hand is still in His. Our heart is still obedient. But now He has led us out of the frightening darkness, with only the pressure of His hand to reassure us, into the sunlight. We look into the Face beside us with a thrill of recognition—the hand of the Father is Jesus' hand!

All along, our heart told us it was so. Relinquishment? Faith? Just daring to trust Jesus.

I RELINQUISH THIS TO YOU

Father, for such a long time I have pleaded before You this, the deep desire of my heart: _____
_____. Yet the more I've clamored for Your help with this, the more remote You have seemed.

I confess my demanding spirit in this matter. I've tried suggesting to You ways my prayer could be answered. To my shame, I've even bargained with You. Yet I know that trying to manipulate the Lord of the Universe is utter foolishness. No wonder my spirit is so sore and weary!

I want to trust You, Father. My spirit knows that these verities are forever trustworthy even when I *feel* nothing . . . .

> That You are there.
>> (You said, "Lo, I am with you alway.") [5]
>
> That You love me.
>> (You said, "I have loved thee with an everlasting love.") [6]
>
> That You alone know what is best for me.
>> (For in You, Lord, "are hid all the treasures of wisdom and knowledge.") [7]

Perhaps all along, You have been waiting for me to give up self-effort. At last I want You in my life even more than I want _____. So now, by an act of my will I relinquish this to You. I will accept Your will, whatever that may be. Thank You for counting this act of my will as the decision of the real person even when my emotions protest. I ask You to hold me true to this decision. To You, Lord God, who alone are worthy of worship, I bend the knee with thanksgiving that this too will "work together for good." [8] *Amen.*

CHAPTER SIX

THE PRAYER
IN SECRET

In the summer of 1960—when I saw for the first time the Sistine Chapel in Rome—I was intrigued to learn something of the working habits of Michelangelo Buonarroti. The four years that it took the great Florentine to paint the vault of the chapel were largely spent in isolation behind locked doors. While very young, Michelangelo had found that for him, work of integrity was impossible without secrecy.

Learning this reminded me again of the power that lies in secrecy. It was in connection with my first book, *A Man Called Peter*,[1] that I experienced its validity. After a rough outline had been approved by the publishers, some instinct told me that until the book was completed, the work should be kept as secret as possible.

Looking back now, I can see at least two reasons why this secrecy was right. I knew that the creativity necessary for the

61

writing was a delicate plant indeed. It could easily wither and die under discouragement or nonconstructive criticism.

I also knew that the ideas of others might cloud my own, could dull and confuse those deepest inner convictions that had to be followed for writing integrity.

Many another writer has found that when he shares an idea for an article or a book too soon, his ability to get the idea on paper sharply deteriorates.

Ernest Hemingway, for instance, has described the trouble he plunged himself into while working on the manuscript of *The Sun Also Rises*. The setting was the village of Schruns in the Austrian Alps. Around the fireside of a winter's evening, Hemingway made the mistake of reading aloud portions of his novel. The danger to him was not negative criticism, rather damage to his own critical judgment through too much unthinking praise, as he describes in *A Moveable Feast:*

> When they said, "It's great, Ernest. Truly, it's great," I wagged my tail in pleasure . . . instead of thinking, "If they . . . like it, what is wrong with it?" That was what I would think if I had been functioning as a professional— although if I had been functioning as a professional, I would never have read it to them.[2]

It was after I had discovered the power of secrecy in the arts that I realized its strength in the equally creative realm of prayer.

In the Sermon on the Mount, Jesus reveals the mysterious spiritual power in secrecy: "But when thou doest alms, let not thy left hand know what thy right hand doeth: That thine alms may be in secret: and thy Father which seeth in secret himself shall reward thee openly." [3]

In addition to charitable giving and good deeds, Jesus applied the principle specifically to two other areas—prayer [4] and spiritual disciplines such as fasting.[5]

One man who took these words literally was George Müller. The result was a story of prayer power that amazed the world. Müller, a German with a practical businessman's mind, was seized with the conviction that he should establish orphanages in nineteenth-century England where there were few provisions for homeless children.

Especially astounding in view of his business background, was the way in which Müller determined to raise the money for this project—by secret prayer. His associates were appalled when he spelled out some of the details:

- No funds would be solicited directly. The method for obtaining contributions would be by prayer *alone*. No worker could give out information about specific needs.

- Names of contributors would also be kept secret. They would be thanked privately. Nor would prominent names ever be used to advertise the institution.

- In spite of these seemingly unpromising preconditions, no debts were to be incurred—all transactions were strictly cash.

George Müller then set aside one hour each day for prayer. As punctually as a Swiss watch, George would retire to his room at the allotted time. On his knees he could concentrate on meeting his Lord, pouring out to God his wishes and hopes and dreams for his work and the needs of his orphans. Once every week, he met with all his associates in a session of prayer—also behind closed doors.

There was something so irresistibly challenging about Müller's formula that despite his aversion to publicity, the news traveled and purses were eagerly opened. Starting with one rented house, two workers, and forty-three children, in time there were five new buildings and 110 workers for 2,050 orphans. In all, during his lifetime, 121,000 orphans were sheltered, fed, educated—a million and a half pounds sterling administered. (Müller kept careful records of every transaction.) The work is still going on as a monument to faith. And at its heart was the Prayer in Secret.

As we walk with Jesus through the Gospel narratives, we find Him acting on this principle Himself. On one occasion when He had just healed a leper, we are told that "Jesus sent him away . . . with the strict injunction, 'Mind you say nothing at all to anybody.'" [6] At another time, when Jesus had raised Jairus's twelve-year-old daughter, we read that her restoration sent her parents almost "out of their minds with joy. But Jesus gave them strict instructions not to let anyone know what had happened . . . ." [7]

The Prayer in Secret need not conflict with praying two-by-two or with small-group prayer. When Jesus raised Jairus's daughter, there were seven persons in the room—the girl, the child's parents, Peter, James, and John, and Christ. Yet following such a group experience, Jesus seems to say that additional power is released if there is no gossip about it outside the prayer room.

When I first read these accounts of Christ's ministry, I assumed that He wanted certain miracles kept secret lest He not be able to cope with the eager crowds or because this might speed Him on His way to the Cross prematurely. But I believe that a more significant reason is involved—that answers to prayer can be diminished, even nullified, by exposing the experience to the comments of the unbelieving. When Jesus returned to His hometown, Nazareth, where the townspeople thought of Him merely as the local carpenter's son, we are told: "And he did not many mighty works there because of their unbelief." [8]

Since this happened to Christ Himself, then how much more easily it could happen to any of us!

How Jesus loved to pray in secret Himself! He had a habit of "rising up a great while before day" and going outdoors—to a mountainside or some other deserted place—to pray. Perhaps because of the small, crowded Palestinian houses, that was the only way He could find privacy and solitude.

Before major decisions—such as His choosing of the twelve apostles—He would pray alone an entire night. And going back to the beginning of His public ministry, we find Jesus going off into the desert for forty days and forty nights of seclusion and concentrated prayer. He knew that power was needed; in secret He would find it.

There are other reasons why Jesus instructs us to pray in secret. Real power in prayer flows only when man's spirit touches God's Spirit. As in worship, so in prayer: "God is a Spirit: and they that worship him must worship him in spirit and in truth." [9] Secrecy helps us get rid of hindrances to praying with our spirit. For instance, in our room with the door shut, we are not so likely to strut and pose and pretend as we are when another human being is present. We know that we cannot deceive God. Transparent honesty before Him is easier for us in isolation.

Then too, there is the necessity of shutting out distractions— the doorbell, the telephone, the laundryman, the children. God asks that we worship Him with concentrated minds as well as allowing the Spirit to direct our wills and emotions. A divided and scattered mind is not at its most receptive.

There is also the matter of our spiritual balance sheets.
When we perform a good deed, we are usually quick to advertise it, display it, collect the credit—use it up. Unworthy or bad
deeds we hide. The "credit" (i.e. debit) of the bad acts stays
with us, accumulates. Thus our personalities are always on the
debit side. Spiritually we remain chronically bankrupt.

Jesus told us that if we want to become fulfilled and produc-
tive persons, we must reverse the process. That is, we are to
divest ourselves of weaknesses, faults, and sins by confessing
them openly, while kindnesses and good deeds are to be kept
secret. The result is an inner reservoir of power.

As the reservoir begins to fill, we experience the Father's
"reward" as promised by Jesus: God's presence in our life and
affairs with all the attendant blessings.

What these blessings turn out to be can be shared with others
only long after our Prayer in Secret has been answered. That is
why I can now tell about our prayer for the Stowe family. (Of
course, this is not their real name.)

It happened one autumn when our children were small. We
knew Mr. Stowe because he was a schoolteacher in our son's
school, a man who gave all of himself to his profession. As
such, he symbolized to us all those unsung citizens who serve
selflessly but often with small pay. The Stowes had five children,
lived in a house too small for such a large family, and were
having a hard time making it financially. Yet they could always
be counted on for community projects. But we knew that they
themselves had too few of the necessities and none of those
extras of the good life that some of us take for granted.

Our concern took the form of dinner-table conversations followed later on by some prayer for the Stowes during one of our
Family Times. Then we asked the question, "Lord, is there
anything You would like *us* to do for the Stowes?"

The answer was not long in coming. We were directed back to an old novel we had all but forgotten, Lloyd C. Douglas's *The Magnificent Obsession*. As we refreshed our minds about the story, we remembered that Randolph, a sculptor, found that when he gave money away as Jesus instructed in the Sermon on the Mount, without letting anyone discover his generous action, power flowed into his life through new energy in his work, fresh sureness and poise in relationships with people, and answered prayers. The sculptor's petition was not for money or fame, but rather for his work: ". . . the capacity to do just one credible work of statuary."

Randolph's prayer was abundantly answered—he became a gifted sculptor. Eventually in fact, fame and material benefits followed as well.

In Douglas's book the "secret of keeping a secret" was then passed on to others—including a brain surgeon—with equally startling results.

All of this led to our deciding to make the Stowes' Christmas a family project, and to keep this a secret from the Stowes as from everyone else.

Other ground rules were laid down: We were to make as many of the presents as possible—like cakes and cookies from cherished old recipes, sequined and beribboned Christmas ornaments; a tiny Christmas tree for the birds, decorated with eatable goodies for them. In addition, our children were to save or earn the money for at least one gift for each of the Stowes.

By Christmas Eve a large carton was filled to the brim with gifts. Attached was a note explaining to our friends that these gifts were to try to say to them how much their continual unselfish giving had meant to many in the community; that since this gift was from the Christ Child Himself, other names were not needed. With each gift went a prayer for God's abundant blessing on their family. The box was then left on the Stowes' doorstep.

And the giving and Prayer in Secret was marvelously answered. Word came to us that the Stowes had one of the greatest Christmases of their lives. Not long after that, Mr. Stowe was offered a better position with a larger salary. Suddenly, the whole community began to show more appreciation for the Stowes' selfless service. The children found various ways to go to college. Blessings for all of us came out of the experience.

Because the prime condition of this prayer *is* secrecy, illustrations beyond one's personal experience with it are not easily come by.

It was only after Janet Ritter's death (not her real name, since we cannot violate her secret either) that members of her family and close friends discovered what a powerful factor the Prayer in Secret had been in her life.

Janet was married to a successful New York journalist. In her forties she became an alcoholic. The best professional care could not cure her. Her defeat and self-loathing took a curious form. Often her husband would come home to their Park Avenue apartment to find his wife unconscious on the floor of her closet. Obsessed by a feeling of guilt during her drinking, Janet would often decide to clean out her closet. She would work at it desperately until she passed out. In the end, the closet held the clue to Janet's release. From the little that Janet told us, we have been able to piece the story together. . . .

On a particular day, she lay across her bed fighting a desperate inner battle. Thanks to Alcoholics Anonymous, she had been dry for two months. That morning she had an overwhelming urge for just one drink. She well knew that once she had one, a hundred more would never be enough. "God help me," she cried. "I can't let my husband and children down again."

On the nightstand beside her was a Bible bound in white leather—little used. That day, however, she opened the Bible by chance to the Sermon on the Mount. Her eyes fell on the word *closet* . . . . Instantly her attention was arrested. Closet! Her closet had become a symbol to her, a hated symbol.

But thou, when thou prayest, enter into thy closet, and when thou hast shut thy door, pray to thy Father which is in secret; and thy Father which seeth in secret shall reward thee openly.[10]

Pray in the closet? Why? Janet had no idea why. But that closet drew her as a magnet. Once again she found herself huddling in among her belongings. Only this time, she was praying, praying for release from her bondage.

The open reward that Jesus promised was given to Janet Ritter. She overcame her temptation for alcohol. In addition, her personality took on such magnetism that, five years after her death, I have seen the faces of friends glow when they speak of her.

Many of the details of her story we shall never uncover. We do know that after that morning, Jesus' formula for power became Janet's guide. She found that giving part of herself or her possessions, in secret, formed the base for rejuvenating her life.

Here are two incidents that came out inadvertently. A private school in New York was instructed to select a worthy girl from a slum district. She would be sent to school, all expenses paid. She must never know her benefactor.

A New York bachelor friend, ill with bronchitis, had a tureen of delicious soup and a tray of delicacies delivered to his door each day. The messenger gave no name; there was no name on the tray. In this case, the bachelor guessed and finally made Janet admit it.

Undoubtedly there was a long series of kindnesses—large and small—all kept secret. The rewards were so open that Janet Ritter's influence for good will go on and on. In addition, to an amazing degree, her personality took on that indefinable feminine charm and magnetism for which every woman longs.

If you feel that your prayers are ineffective, as we all do at times, I suggest you explore the formula for prayer that Jesus bequeathed to us. The world desperately needs the concentrated power that comes from praying in secret.

OUR SECRET

Father, I begin to see that You have decreed the Law of Secrecy all through Your Creation. Seeds secreted in the warm earth are invisible to all eyes but Yours during the long days of germination. Baby chicks hidden in the eggs do not cackle or crow during the weeks of incubation beneath the patient mother hen. Our creation too requires the months of seclusion in the dark of the womb. So I see that prayer, the highest form of creation, must also for a time be hidden with You for Your work to be accomplished.

Lord, here is a request dear to my heart: _____ _____. It strengthens my faith to know that You want this petition to be our secret; that as I hide my request in You, I have touched the creative heart of the universe.

So I leave this prayer with You, Father. As day follows day with no results visible to me, give me the gift of knowing that since You care for me more tenderly than for any seeds or eggs, Your work of Creation on my behalf is going on just as surely. How I thank You! In the beauty and strength of Jesus' name I pray. *Amen.*

A suggestion: for most of us a bit of dramatization helps. You could write out your Prayer in Secret, date it, and insert it between the pages of a little-used Bible close to a promise that speaks to you, such as Matthew 6:3, 4. Then leave it there until your prayer is answered. C.M.

CHAPTER SEVEN

THE PRAYER OF
JOYOUS BLESSING

Some years ago, I knew of a home in Washington, D.C., which was full of tension because of an aunt's nagging faultfinding with the children. Ellen R——, the mother of the family, did much praying about this situation, mostly that God would take away the aunt's hypercritical attitude. Nothing at all seemed to happen as a result, and Ellen became increasingly resentful of the aunt's attitude and presence in her home.

One afternoon, Ellen—whom I had known for many years—dropped by our home to return a borrowed book.

"I know I must look a wreck," she apologized. "I feel like a ball knocked back and forth between the children and Auntie."

In the midst of discussing her problem, I had a sudden inspiration. "You've been asking God to change your aunt's disposition, and you say she's more faultfinding than ever. So why not forget about trying to change your aunt and just ask God to bless her—in anything and everything?"

Ellen looked astonished. "You mean I should ask God to bless Auntie whether she deserves it or not?"

Before I could answer, my friend had a counter thought. "I see it," Ellen said thoughtfully. "I guess none of us *deserves* anything from God, do we?"

"That's exactly my thought," I told Ellen. "Nothing we could ever do would be good enough to earn a scrap or a rag from His hands."

"Then, Catherine, let's try your idea. But will you pray with me about it right now?"

"Of course. But remember, Ellen, when you ask God to bless someone, what you're really saying is, 'Make him or her happy.' That's the literal meaning of *blessing* in the Bible—happiness."

As I recall, Ellen's prayer went something like this: "Lord, I know it's Your will that we be happier in our house than we have been. And I know that can't happen while any one of us is unhappy. Bless Auntie now in whatever ways she needs. Give her the gift of happiness. Help the children to love and respect her—and show me how I can be kinder to her. *Amen.*"

A week later my friend telephoned. Ellen said that day by day her prayer was being abundantly answered. "The atmosphere here at home is completely different. You know this blessing business is dynamite! But I still don't understand why that prayer was answered when none of the others were. Why would there be such power in wishing joy for someone?"

Perhaps one reason we are surprised when God moves to bless someone when we ask it, is that we have thought of Jesus Christ as primarily "a man of sorrows, and acquainted with grief." [1] No man with an attitude of gloom could ever have drawn little children to Him. Only an enthusiastic man who went out to meet life with unflagging zest could have attracted rugged fishermen as His disciples. Sadness couldn't last long when a man delightedly threw away his crutches or a leper went off leaping and singing on his way to show his clean new flesh to the priest. And don't forget that the Gospels record Jesus as breaking up every funeral He attended!

Certainly, Jesus was unblinkingly aware of life's problems and disappointments: "In the world ye shall have tribulation," He promised His disciples. "But," He added, "be of good cheer; I have overcome the world." [2] Or in other words, "Cheer up! The worst that the world can do is no match for Me."

The real source of Jesus' joy is given us in unforgettable words first spoken by the Psalmist [3] and centuries later by the author of Hebrews:

Thou [Christ] hast loved righteousness, and hated iniquity; therefore God, even thy God, hath anointed thee with the oil of gladness above thy fellows. [4]

He who knew no sin and *is* righteousness, had a personality sparkling and overflowing with a degree of gladness which none of us can match. How could it be otherwise!

That's why the Prayer of Joyous Blessing does not depend on our merit or lack of it. Jesus is the *only* righteous One, therefore the only finally joyous One. But this joy He longs to share with all who will receive it.

Now we begin to see why my friend Ellen was on firm ground in not making her aunt's "worthiness" a condition for her Prayer of Joyous Blessing. She knew that Jesus has told us: "Love your enemies . . . Bless them that curse you." [5]

As soon as we begin to obey Him, we find that blessing those with whom we are having difficulties and the *answer* to these difficulties, go hand in hand.

I had this connection between the Prayer of Joyous Blessing and God's power to transform situations dramatized for me some years ago when a woman came to see me, asking my advice about her marriage. Over a cup of tea she told me her problem. She had just had the hardest blow the feminine ego can sustain—her husband had announced that he no longer loved her and was going to leave her.

Mrs. B____ felt that their marital problems were her husband's fault and she was full of harsh criticism of him—he never went to church; he spent little time with their children; he was unfaithful. "Only God can save him," Mrs. B____ intoned gloomily.

"Here's an idea how to pray for your husband," I suggested. "Ask God to rain His blessings—spiritual, physical, and material—on him, and leave the rest to God."

My visitor sipped her tea, and her lips pursed into a firmer line. "My husband has prospered too much already," she said. "That's the trouble with him. The only thing that will ever bring him to his senses and back to God is trouble, and more trouble."

She left, saying that she was going to pray that God would change her husband, make him good, then bring him back to her and the children. And her prayers fell to the ground. The husband eventually got a divorce and married someone else.

In one of His parables, Jesus left us His comments about Mrs. B____'s kind of prayer for her husband. One day Jesus had watched two men praying in the Temple—an important, well-educated Pharisee and a lowly publican. "Don't do as the Pharisee," the Master later told His disciples. "His prayer was, 'I thank thee that I am not as other men are—extortioners, unjust, adulterers, or even as this publican.' " [6]

Then Jesus threw in the wry suggestion that the Pharisee was not "praying" at all, he was talking to himself. Of course he did not go down to his house "justified," [7] that is, his prayer was not answered.

Why not? Because God hears not what our lips say, but what we really mean behind the facade of words. So what did the Pharisee mean? Something like this: "Lord, I thank Thee that I'm not like Mr. _____. I am good; this other person is bad. He does not deserve Your blessings. I suggest that You send this sinner a lot of trouble. That ought to bring him to his senses. It won't do, Lord, to have the wicked prosper."

If you and I were running the world, probably we would not allow the wicked to prosper. But the simple truth is that often they do prosper. All through the centuries, this fact has bothered men. In what may be the oldest book in the Bible, Job wrestles with the problem. It is mentioned in Psalm after Psalm. But Jesus was and always is the Realist. He simply took it for granted that because God is all love, the wicked *will* often prosper: ". . . for he maketh his sun to rise on the evil and on the good, and sendeth rain on the just and on the unjust." [8]

"Therefore," said Jesus, "if you are going to be true sons of your Father in heaven, then you'll have to pray for the very best to happen to everyone you know—no matter how you personally may have been mistreated or hurt by them." [9]

Is Jesus saying then, that goodness or wickedness are of no consequence to God? Not at all! Sin is a serious matter, serious enough to have sent Christ to His Cross, and our world closer and closer to the brink of disaster. But the point is that self-righteous prayers or accusing prayers do not change men from bad to good. Only joyous love redeems.

Our Dutch friend, Corrie ten Boom, was trying hard to obey Jesus by loving her enemies one night in a Munich church. She

had just finished her talk when she spied him—a former German
S.S. guard especially loathed by the prisoners in the concentra-
tion camp at Ravensbruck. This man had been one of many
who had "despitefully used" Corrie and her sister Betsie during
their imprisonment there. Betsie had died in this camp. After
Corrie was released in late 1945, she went about the former
enemy country of Germany speaking out to all who would
listen, the message that God had laid on her heart like a live
coal—forgiveness.

And now here he was, the first of her actual jailers whom
Corrie had seen since her release. This was the man with the
leering face and the mocking voice who had stood guard at the
shower-room door in Ravensbruck. Corrie's heart sank as she
saw the man coming towards her.

"Fraulein," he said ingratiatingly, extending his hand, "thank
you for your message. To think that He has washed our sins
away!"

Corrie felt her right arm go stiff, ramrod straight against her
side. Even as a storm of angry, vengeful thoughts boiled up
inside her, she knew how wrong they were. She who had just
finished talking about loving our enemies, was being asked to
make good her words.

She tried to smile, struggled to raise her arm, but she could
not. Her heart felt no trace of warmth for the man standing
there with his hand extended.

"Jesus, I cannot forgive him," went her quick inward prayer.
"Give me *Your* forgiveness." Then Corrie's arm reached out
and as her fingers touched the man's, incredibly, she felt something like an electric current begin at her shoulder, race along
her arm and pass into the German. Simultaneously, into her
heart sprang such a joyful love for the former guard as she
would not have believed possible.[10] Thereafter, Corrie found

that she *could* pray with ease that God would rain abundant blessings on the former guard.

That's the way Corrie ten Boom discovered what all of us have to come to sooner or later: We can love our "enemy" enough to ask gladness for him, only if He who was anointed with so much gladness, does it for us.

Long before Jesus' day, the ancient Israelites had stumbled on the truth that gladness is a key to God's presence: *The joy of the Lord is your strength . . . . In thy presence is fulness of joy . . . . Serve the Lord with gladness: come before His presence with singing.*[11]

As he wrote his Psalms, perhaps David was remembering the day he had literally come into God's presence with singing —and dancing. Israel's standing enemies, the Philistines, had finally been defeated. The sacred ark could now safely be brought to Jerusalem. So David had brought it: "With gladness . . . he danced before the Lord with all his might . . . with shouting and the sound of the trumpet." [12]

And Michal, his wife, watching his joyous abandon, had been embarrassed. Her husband was making a fool of himself! So she "despised him in her heart." The writer of the old story then adds a curious footnote to the story. Michal was never to have the most fervent desire of her heart granted: she was to remain childless until the day of her death.[13]

Scripture does not explain this further. We can guess that Michal's inability to enter into David's joyousness was merely a symptom of deeper trouble. The queen despised her husband. Like Mrs. B____, she was probably habitually nursing grudges and resentments—prime blockages to answered prayer.

Had Michal been able to forgive, joy could have joined hands with love, perhaps to grant her fervent desire for children along with many another answered prayer.

Agnes Sanford, the Episcopal rector's widow, has told about how she first met the power of joy when her baby had been ill for six weeks with abscessed ears. Her prayers for healing, she said later, had been negated by the fear and desperation in her heart. Then one day a young minister called. "I'll go upstairs and have a prayer with the baby," he offered.

The mother was skeptical about his prayer achieving anything that hers had not, but showed him the way to the baby's room. The young rector tenderly held the baby's head in his big hands. Mrs. Sanford said later, remembering the incident, "Light shone in the minister's eyes. I looked at him and saw his loving joyfulness, and I believed. For joy is the heavenly 'okay' of the inner life of power . . . ." [14]

The baby promptly went to sleep. When he awoke, he was well.

Queen Elizabeth's standard flying over Buckingham Palace in London is the sign that the queen is in residence. Joy looking out of the Christian's eyes is the sign that the King is in residence within. Similarly, in prayer, joy is a sure sign of the King's approval.

It is possible to find the way to pray with joy even in a very serious and seemingly tragic situation. Do we need healing? One way is to ask ourselves why we want health. Then make a series of happy pictures in the mind of the creative ways that we would use health.

Or do we need financial help? How would we use adequate financial resources? One way of joyous prayer is to create a series of pictures in the mind of the way we would use money, not just for ourselves, but to extend His joy to others.

Having so often seen the Prayer of Joyous Blessing gloriously answered, I've begun to wonder recently if here we don't have a key to the problem of world peace. Even for those who take prayer seriously, it isn't easy to know how to pray for other nations. It is especially hard when their ideals are not ours, and when they consider themselves our enemies.

Perhaps Christ would say to us, "The people of all nations are My children, too. The more violent, greedy men ignore Me and prey on My innocents, the more they need to be released to My all-encompassing love."

Now obviously, we cannot bless and pray for people who despitefully use others or with whom we are at odds, unless we recognize that no self-effort can manage this and let Christ—living in us—love others for us.

But it may be that if even a handful of citizens could pray with that kind of joy for the people of "enemy" nations, with the expectation of good, asking for God's all-abundant blessings on them in every sphere—tremendous results would be forthcoming.

Our first reaction to that suggestion may be exactly what Mrs. B____'s was. Too risky! Which of us wants other nations to pull out ahead of our nation in the sciences, in the exploration of outer space, in military know-how, or in the economic sphere?

But it is not a risky way to pray, once we see that God's way is to make "his sun to rise on the just and on the unjust," and that His sun of joy is the only power in the universe capable of transforming the hearts of men—no matter what their problems, their politics, or their nationality.

BLESS US, FATHER

Father, I cringe to see myself in that Pharisee in the Temple,[15] for I have been believing a lie:

> That since I have tried to serve You, I have a right to ask for Your blessings.

> But that _____, so unbelieving and uncaring about You, deserves the difficulties he has.

Now I understand, Father, that You must manifest love and joy to us, Your creatures, because You *are* love and joy; that You, as the Sun of Righteousness in whom no darkness dwells,[16] shine upon us because it is Your nature to shine—not because a one of us is deserving of it.

I now release _____ from my judgment and I ask You to bless him abundantly in any and every way that seems good to You.

So live Your life in me, Lord, that from henceforward I shall desire as much good for others as I ask for myself; that I shall never again plead largess for myself and in my heart begrudge Your blessings for others.

Cleanse me of all selfishness and ungenerosity. And O Father, fill me up with the joy of Him who was anointed with the oil of gladness [17] above us all. In His name, I pray. *Amen.*

CHAPTER EIGHT

THE CLAIMING PRAYER

I first became aware of the Claiming Prayer back in 1947 when I noticed a strange sentence written on the flyleaf of Peter Marshall's Bible . . . .

It's the word of a Gentleman of the most sacred and strictest honour, and there's an end on it!

DAVID LIVINGSTONE

Underneath Livingstone's name, Peter had signed his own.

When I asked Peter for an explanation of the words, he thumped the cover of his Bible and said, "In these pages are the living words of the living God. These words include a lot of promises, many of them with conditions attached. All we have to do is to meet the conditions, then step up and claim them."

He was silent for a moment. Then . . . "Remember how I promised Peter John to take him down to the train store this Saturday?"

I nodded.

"Well, I'd be a poor father if I failed to keep promises like that to my son. And if I'm conscientious enough to want to keep my word, how much more so is God!"

"But that quote in the front of your Bible," I reminded him, "is there a story behind it?"

There was, and Peter referred me to the missionary's journals. It was 1856. Livingstone faced one of the gravest perils of his sixteen years in Africa. He was passing through the wild country of the native chief, Mburuma, who was hostile and had been seeking to rouse the countryside against the white man's expedition. Reports had been coming in that natives were creeping towards the camp.

Alone in his tent, Livingstone opened his Bible to the promise on which he had staked his life so often. Then he wrote in his journal:

> January 14, 1856. Evening. Felt much turmoil of spirit in view of having all my plans for the welfare of this great region and teeming population knocked on the head by savages tomorrow. But I read that Jesus came and said: *All power is given unto Me in heaven and in earth. Go ye therefore, and teach all nations . . . and lo, I am with you alway, even unto the end of the world.* It's the word of a Gentleman of the most sacred and strictest honour, so there's an end on it! I will not cross furtively by night as intended.[1]

Thus Livingstone claimed the promise of Jesus' presence.

During the hours of darkness nothing happened. The next morning Livingstone, still calm, superintended the crossing of the river for his company of 114 men and their riding oxen while Mburuma and his tribesmen watched from the jungle's edge.

The missionary reserved for himself the last place in the last canoe. One native bearer, fearful of treachery, pleaded with Livingstone not to give the chief a chance to shoot him in the back.

"Tell him to observe that I am not afraid," Livingstone replied. Then with dignity he approached the astonished natives, thanked them, wished them God's peace, and walked slowly to the canoe. The crossing was made safely. During those moments the missionary-explorer must have been vividly aware of the One who walked beside him. "Lo, I am with you alway," he had penned the night before. And now faith had become fact: *He,* the Lord, was there beside him.

For the Risen One this was a reenactment of an incident during His days on earth in the flesh. There had been the same kind of seething mob bent on treachery:

. . . they mobbed him and took him to the edge of the hill on which the city was built to push him over the cliff.[2]

But he passing through the midst of them went his way.[3]

The Kingly Presence beside Livingstone gave the missionary such nobility of bearing that even native warriors felt it. Not a hand was raised to molest him.

Livingstone had prayed the Claiming Prayer. For himself and his company, he had claimed Jesus' promise, *Lo, I am with you alway.* And He of the sacred honour had fulfilled His word.

David Livingstone's experience made such an impression on me that those words in Peter's Bible have been associated with the Claiming Prayer ever since.

Yet I had no base on which to use this way of praying until my attitude towards the Bible changed. I began by considering Bible reading a dull chore. College courses in which we studied the Scriptures as literature or in Comparative Religion as simply one of many world religions, had not changed the tedium I felt.

Nor had such courses given me an answer about how I was to regard the Bible. Was it a collection of myths and folklore "inspired" only in the sense that the plays of Shakespeare or the poetry of John Keats were inspired? Or was Scripture the authoritative Word of God Himself, somehow channeled through the minds and pens of certain picked men? I did not know.

But after I made an act of committing my life to God, gradually, for me, the Bible underwent a transformation. I wanted to read the Bible because it told me so much about the character and ways of God. I found myself eager to know how He dealt with men and women in every imaginable circumstance, so that I could have some idea how He would deal with me. And the more I read in this remarkable book, the more surely I knew that in its pages God Himself was speaking to me.

"But *how* do you know that?" I've been asked sometimes. "How can you be certain?"

My answer came out of the dawning realization that we human beings arrive at surety by one of two routes. With questions pertaining to our bodies or material matters, we are convinced by intellectual, scientific, or evidential proof. With questions pertaining to man's spirit, we are convinced only by personal revelation. For instance, a question like, "How do I know He loves me?" can never be proved by reasoning or in the laboratory. For love is in the area of spirit from whose door the scientific kind of proof is turned away every time. Yet the flooding inner revelation: "He *does* love me! He loves *me!*" is valid, bringing such surety that I am willing to commit my life to my love.

When we realize the range of important questions which will always elude the net of final intellectual or scientific proof, then we begin to appreciate the significance of revelation. Surely, here is a most important gift we should ask for more often.

One of my friends, who like me arrived at this place of surety via personal revelation, likes to think of the Bible this way:

> The Scriptures *are* letters—personal letters from God to each one of us. If you want to open your mail, just read through any of the passages that begin with the word *whosoever*—and substitute the words "that means me" for *whosoever*. These are the promises God has made to each one of us . . . . And we can take God at His Word! [4]

"We can take God at His Word," says Colleen Townsend Evans in *Love Is an Everyday Thing*. "The word of a Gentleman of the most sacred and strictest honour," David Livingstone wrote. Once we too *know* like that, then we understand something else—that God means that all lives be lived in cooperation with Him. His friendship, His plans for us, His riches are awaiting each of us, provided we want Him in our lives and tell Him so.

And then the point of the Claiming Prayer becomes clear—the riches of grace must be claimed. ". . . *ye have not, because ye ask not*," the Apostle James cried. [5]

The process goes like this:

- God has made a promise.

- If there are conditions attached to it, we do our best to meet them.

- We make an act of claiming this promise at a specific time and place.

- God fulfills the promise in His own time and His own
  way.

How practical the Claiming Prayer can be was illustrated by
a series of incidents told me some years ago by my longtime
friend Colleen, the wife of Louis Evans, the pastor of the Na-
tional Presbyterian Church in the nation's capital.

Colleen had been a rising movie star. For years, tutors, studio
cars, the services of makeup men, and glamorous clothes had
been at her disposal.

Before marrying Louis, Colleen made the decision to give up
her movie career. In the years since, despite some tempting
offers, she has never compromised with that decision. But little
did Colleen know how difficult the transition would be.

Four years after their marriage, Louis was asked to start a
new church in the Los Angeles suburb of Bel Air. He accepted
the challenge. His salary was quite inadequate for a wife and
by then, three young children, the needs of a manse, money for
the constant entertaining necessary, and ministerial books. Thus
no paid household help was possible.

At the end of the first year in the new parish, Coke—as her
friends call her—felt herself at the end of all physical and
spiritual resources. Always tired, she could never see over the
top of a mountain of home chores (since with no building, their
home was the church) and church work. Nor could she even find
time for a few minutes of quietness and prayer. She felt utterly
exhausted and knew that she needed help.

Coke's first opportunity to think through the situation came
during the family's summer vacation. Away from the parish and
the tyranny of the telephone, with the children playing outdoors
most of the days, she determined to pray her way through to
some answers. She placed before God three acute problems:

- There was simply too much work. She felt like a servant in her own home. How could one woman be maid, cook, laundress, mother, wife, as well as church janitor?

- Constant interruptions from parishioners and friends through visits and telephone calls.

- The need for a daily Quiet Time. How could she manage that?

"That summer God gave me insight into every problem," Coke told me. "He answered me with words from Scripture that were manna to my spirit. He didn't pamper me or take away my difficulties, but He showed me how to make a new beginning in handling each situation by claiming His strength."

These are the answers Coke received:

For feeling like a servant in her own home: "I mean for My children to minister, to be servants in every way.[6] Accept your role. The important thing is your willingness to pick it up. Then I will do the rest. Above all, do not feel sorry for yourself." Jesus also counted Himself servant of all.[7]

For too much work: No one has ever had a nervous breakdown just from overwork; it is the worrying about tomorrow and next week that is making your load unbearable. Claim My strength one day at a time with the promise: *And as thy days, so shall thy strength be.*[8] Also learn to say *no* sometimes. Ask yourself, "Is this what people want, or what my Father wants?"

When interruptions come: Treat them as Jesus did. There were many times when He yearned to be left alone too. Yet He reacted to interruptions not by resisting or resenting them, but by accepting and using them as opportunities to teach and help people.[9] He understands your situation because He had it much worse. Claim His help in treating your interruptions His way.

Finding a Quiet Time: With young children in the home

there will be few uninterrupted stretches of time. So watch for
free minutes, chinks of time throughout the day to pray. The
question really is, how much do you *want* to pray? Claim this
promise for the quiet heart: *For God is not the author of confusion, but of peace* . . . .[10]

Now, years later, there is abundant evidence how bounti-
fully Colleen Evans's Claiming Prayers were answered. Though
the children are older, there are still interruptions. Yet the old
desperation and threat of a breakdown have long since given
way to a quiet effectiveness. Rarely have I seen a more successful wife, mother, and minister's helpmate. To crown it all, Coke
is still a glamorously beautiful woman. By now the author of two
books, she even finds time to serve on the board of trustees of
two outstanding educational institutions.

I believe the Claiming Prayer to be the crown of all ways of
prayer because it inscribes a completed circle between earth and
heaven, thus meeting the conditions of prayer power. For the
purpose of all prayer is to find God's will and to make that will
our prayer, so that as Jesus bade us pray in the Lord's Prayer,
the Father's will may be done as perfectly on earth as it is in
heaven.

Thus we go to God with a problem, seeking light on it. We
give God a chance to speak to us either through Scripture or
through His quiet voice in our hearts. This part makes half of
the circle as our need sweeps up to God.

Then God points out to us one of His promises which applies
to our situation. Our claiming of this promise will complete the
circle—from heaven to earth.

This promise is the handle of faith that we can grasp in prayer.
The Apostle John has expressed it in words of pure gold:

And this is the confidence that we have in him, that, if we ask anything according to his will, he heareth us: And if we know that he hear us, whatsoever we ask, we know that we have the petitions that we desired of him.[11]

Strange, how one's mind and spirit leap in joyful response to John's words. "Yes, John, you're right. I see it! Of course God is going to grant me what has been His will for me all along." So in that faith we make a specific act of claiming the promise that God Himself has given us.

If there are any conditions attached to this promise, we do our best to meet them, for He who will not let us down also will not let us off. To illustrate: the condition of having our sins cleansed is our forgiveness of others;[12] the condition of material blessing is that we give priority to the Kingdom of God;[13] one condition for guidance is acknowledging God in every area of our lives;[14] and the condition for world peace is high: humbling ourselves as a nation, praying, and turning from evil.[15]

After that, we wait for the fulfillment of the promise, secure in the knowledge of a God who cannot lie,[16] and that he who believes in Him will never be disappointed.[17]

The Claiming Prayer is the most incisive way of prayer that I know, resting its case as it does on that "word of a Gentleman of the most sacred and strictest honour."

Try it. He will never fail you.

I CLAIM YOUR PROMISE

Father, with my mind I have tried to understand You and Your ways. But the confusion and uncertainty in my life dramatize how limited my capacity for understanding is. I see now why You have provided us, Your creatures, with an added dimension beyond intelligence: an inner spirit to be a receiving set for Your Spirit. Father, if ever anyone needed the revelation of Spirit, I do. I ask now for the illumination that is the Spirit's gift of revelation about . . . .

the Bible and how I should read it. (Is it really Your Word in a special sense?)

the particular promise from Scripture You want to give me today.

Father, I see how this promise relates to this situation:

_____

_____. In faith, I copy these "words of a Gentleman" on a slip of paper.[18]

And now, Father, I claim them for myself and my situation by endorsing it on the back. How grateful I am that this check is signed by Him whose integrity is impeccable. I rest on the sure knowledge that behind this check stands final security—all the resources and reserves of heaven. Thank You, Father. *Amen.*

NOTES

Chapter 1   Prayer Is Asking

1. Luke 15:8–10.
2. James 4:2 MOFFATT.
3. Matthew 20:29–34 MOFFATT.
4. Matthew 7:11 MOFFATT (*italics* added).
5. Matthew 7:7, 8 MOFFATT (*italics* added).
6. John 16:24 MOFFATT (*italics* added).
7. Luke 11:11, 12.
8. Mark 10:15 LB.
9. Luke 18:9–14 RSV.
10. C. S. Lewis, *The Screwtape Letters* (New York: The Macmillan Co., 1943), p. 21.
11. John R. Rice, *Asking and Receiving* (Wheaton, Ill.: Sword of the Lord Publishers, 1942), p. 50.
12. John 4:5–30.

Chapter 2   The Prayer of Helplessness

1. Psalms 4:1 MOFFATT.
2. John 15:5.
3. John 5:30, 36.
4. John 6:44 MOFFATT.
5. Ephesians 2:8, 9.
6. John 3:27.
7. Brother Lawrence, *Conversations: The Practice of the Presence of God* (Old Tappan, N.J.: Fleming H. Revell Co., 1973), pp. 15, 16.
8. Matthew 19:26.
9. A. B. Simpson, *The Gospel of Healing* (Harrisburg, Pa.: Christian Publishers, 1915), pp. 169 ff.
10. Adapted from "The Hound of Heaven," from *Complete Poetical Works of Francis Thompson* (New York: Boni and Liveright, Inc.), p. 93. The poem reads: "Is my gloom, after all, Shade of His hand, outstretched caressingly?"

Chapter 3   The Prayer That Helps Your Dreams Come True

1. Proverbs 29:18.
2. 1 John 5:14, 15.

Chapter 4   The Waiting Prayer

1. A favorite illustration of Peter Marshall's. He used it to help answer the question, "How much should I do to help God answer my prayers, and how much should I leave with Him?" Catherine Marshall, *A Man Called Peter* (New York: McGraw-Hill Book Company, 1951), pp. 180, 181.
2. John 15:1–8.
3. Mark 4:28.
4. Mark 1:15.
5. John 7:6.
6. Matthew 26:18.
7. Acts 1:7.
8. Lamentations 3:25.
9. Psalms 37:9.
10. Isaiah 40:31.
11. Isaiah 64:4 LB
12. Galatians 6:9.

Chapter 5   The Prayer of Relinquishment

1. Mark 14:36 PHILLIPS.
2. Luke 6:46.
3. Matthew 5:39.
4. Ephesians 2:8; 1 Corinthians 12:9.
5. Matthew 28:20.
6. Jeremiah 31:3.
7. Colossians 2:3.
8. Romans 8:28.

Chapter 6   The Prayer in Secret

1. Catherine Marshall, *A Man Called Peter* (New York: McGraw-Hill Book Company, 1951).
2. Ernest Hemingway, *A Moveable Feast* (New York: Charles Scribner's Sons, 1964), p. 209.
3. Matthew 6:3, 4.
4. Matthew 6:5, 6.
5. Matthew 6:16–18.
6. Mark 1:43, 44 PHILLIPS.
7. Mark 5:42, 43 PHILLIPS.
8. Matthew 13:58.
9. John 4:24.
10. Matthew 6:6.

Chapter 7   The Prayer of Joyous Blessing

1. Isaiah 53:3.
2. John 16:33.
3. Psalms 45:7.
4. Hebrews 1:9.
5. Luke 6:27, 28.
6. Luke 18:11.
7. Luke 18:14.
8. Matthew 5:45.
9. Matthew 5:44; Luke 6:28 (paraphrased).
10. Corrie ten Boom, *The Hiding Place* (Washington Depot, Conn.: Chosen Books, 1971), p. 215.
11. Nehemiah 8:10; Psalms 16:11; 100:2.
12. 2 Samuel 6:14–16.
13. 2 Samuel 6:20–23.
14. Agnes Sanford, *The Healing Light* (St. Paul, Minn.: Macalester Park Publishing Company, 1971), pp. 17, 18.
15. Luke 18:11.
16. 1 John 1:5.
17. Hebrews 1:9.

Chapter 8   The Claiming Prayer

1. Isaac Schapera, ed., *Livingstone's African Journal 1853–1856*, 2 vols. (London: Chatto and Windus Ltd., 1963), Vol. II, p. 374.
2. Luke 4:29 LB
3. Luke 4:30.
4. Colleen Townsend Evans, *Love Is an Everyday Thing* (Old Tappan, N.J.: Fleming H. Revell Co., 1974), p. 120.
5. James 4:2.
6. Mark 10:44.
7. Mark 10:45.
8. Deuteronomy 33:25.
9. Mark 6:31–46.
10. 1 Corinthians 14:33.
11. 1 John 5:14, 15.
12. Matthew 6:14, 15.
13. Matthew 6:33.
14. Proverbs 3:6.
15. 2 Chronicles 7:14.
16. Titus 1:2.
17. 1 Peter 2:6 MOFFATT.
18. It might be helpful to write out on a slip of paper the promise given to you.